Saint Mary Magdalene

SEAN DAVIDSON, M.S.E.

Saint Mary Magdalene

~

Prophetess of Eucharistic Love

IGNATIUS PRESS   SAN FRANCISCO

Cover art:

Saint Mary Magdalene, 1498, Louis Brea
Altarpiece of Saint Margaret's Church of Luceram
Alpes-Maritime, France
Photograph by Father Florian Racine

Monstrance art from iStockphoto.com, © c12

Cover design by Riz Boncan Marsella

© 2017 by Ignatius Press, San Francisco
All rights reserved
ISBN 978-1-62164-092-9
Library of Congress Control Number 2016910797
Printed in the United States of America ∞

Contents

Foreword

As rector of the Basilica of Saint Mary Magdalene, home
to the famous resting place of the Apostle of the Apostles,
I was delighted to be asked to write the foreword for this
book. It is a timely work, because the life of Saint Magdalene bears witness to the infinite mercy of Christ, and
our world stands in great need of an outpouring of divine
mercy today. Its publication coincides perfectly with the
conclusion of the Year of Mercy, a time of grace and renewal for the Church. This work is also timely because
Saint Mary Magdalene was the first herald of the Resurrection of the Lord, and our world stands in great need
of a new evangelisation today. The Good News of the
Risen Christ which was first announced by Mary Magdalene long ago has lost nothing of its saving force. "Jesus
Christ is the same yesterday and today and for ever." (Heb
13:8) The publication of this work also accompanies the
recent decision of the Church to honor the Apostle of the
Apostles with a liturgical feast day rather than a memorial.
Although here in the diocese of Fréjus-Toulon we have
always honored her with a feast day, it is a providential
gift to have that blessing extended to the entire Universal
Church.

Father Davidson has written this book in continuity
with the ancient Catholic tradition on the life of the saint,

but he has done so from a new perspective: in relation to the eucharistic Mystery. His work goes to the heart of the identity of this holy woman who was above all an ardent adorer in spirit and in truth. (Jn 4:23) Before anything else, she is a witness to the transforming power of an encounter with Jesus Christ, an encounter which blossomed into a life of adoration at his feet. Her contemplation and adoration of the Lord Jesus continued until the end of her life in the lonely mountains of Sainte-Baume here in Provence. For this reason, she is the perfect biblical model for those who have encountered Christ, truly present in the Blessed Sacrament, and who seek to deepen their life of adoration at the feet of the eucharistic Lord. Adoration is essentially about love, and in the Gospels there are few people who understood love as well as Saint Mary Magdalene. On page after page of this book, the author draws out her profound secrets of love, through which the adorer can learn how to become ever more pleasing to the Heart of Christ. Cardinal Robert Sarah, prefect of the Congregation for Divine Worship, also grasped the fact that Saint Magdalene is first and foremost a model of adoration. He explained this in the essay which he wrote to celebrate her first feast day in the Church. He said: "St. Mary Magdalene seeks the Lord, and when she finds him, she adores him. . . . Adoration takes first place. Mary Magdalene reminds us of the need to recover the primacy of God and the primacy of adoration in the life of the Church and in the liturgical celebration."[1]

---

[1] Cardinal Robert Sarah, Essay on Saint Mary Magdalene. *L'Osservatore Romano*, Italian Edition, July 22, 2016. Trans. Diane Montagna of Aleteia's English Edition.

Finally, this book paints a beautiful portrait of the merciful Face of Jesus, and it is as much a commentary on the life of Christ as it is on the life of Mary Magdalene. If it makes use of the example of Saint Magdalene as a subject for meditation, it is only so as to draw us into a deeper understanding of the Person of Christ. It is my hope that on these pages many people will find nourishment for their souls and discover anew the timeless figure of the Apostle of the Apostles. May her example enkindle a new fire of love for Christ in our hearts, and may her intercession accompany the reader at every moment.

FATHER FLORIAN RACINE

Rector of the Basilica
of Saint Mary Magdalene,
Saint Maximin-la-Sainte-Baume

Preface

The writing of this short book has been a labour of love. The reason I have felt called to write it is simply that people have asked me to do so. For two years I had the privilege of living in the shadow of the magnificent Basilica of Saint Mary Magdalene in a little town in Provence called Saint Maximin-la-Sainte-Baume. This most ancient site of pilgrimage is the official home of the relics of the Apostle to the Apostles, the great Saint Mary Magdalene. During my time living in this extraordinary place, so rich in grace and beauty, I would often have the joy of welcoming groups of English-speaking pilgrims. As I would explain to them the history of the basilica, along with the biblical and extra-biblical traditions about Saint Mary Magdalene, the response would almost always be something along these lines: "I didn't know any of that." "Why don't we hear about this more often?" "Where can I find a good book on the subject?" My reply to this final question would be that, unfortunately, I do not know of any book in the English language that provides a portrait of the saint as she has always been depicted in that sanctuary.

All of the great works on Saint Mary Magdalene that I know of are in French. (Perhaps there are some books of this kind in English, but I would have difficulty in providing the name of one.) I considered perhaps translating one of the books written by Henri Lacordaire, Pierre de Bérulle or a more modern work by Jean-Pierre Ravotti. In the end, however, I decided to take the more audacious step of putting on paper what I have come to accept as a faithful image of her who has become one of my favourite saints.

During my time in Saint Maximin I would use the scriptural texts traditionally associated with Saint Mary Magdalene as an inspiration for my holy hours and the talks I would give on eucharistic adoration. She is a true model of adoration and provides us with examples of the four pillars of eucharistic prayer: namely, adoration, thanksgiving, reparation and intercession. This book is the fruit of much time spent with Saint Mary Magdalene before the Most Blessed Sacrament. Perhaps it will help others to enter into a eucharistic meditation of this beautiful disciple of Christ. I write it in the spirit of the brothers of Saint Dominic who for almost seven hundred years were the custodians of the basilica that houses the precious relics of this dear friend of Jesus Christ. Their entire mission consisted in "passing on to others what they themselves had contemplated". So along with what I have learned from my happy time spent in Provence, I now pass on to you some thoughts on Saint Mary Magdalene that I have received for the most part before the eucharistic face of Jesus.

INTRODUCTION

The Happy Ending of a
Beautiful Love Story

A most ancient oral tradition tells us that a large group of Christ's intimate friends were exiled from their homeland during the first persecutions of the Christians in Jerusalem, in or around the year A.D. 41. Exile was a tactic often employed by persecutors in the ancient world to avoid the complications of martyrdom and to rid their regions of the unstoppable influence of the saints. Already in the Gospel of John we hear how the Pharisees were considering putting Lazarus to death because his resurrection would lead to "the world" going after Christ (Jn 12:19). In the end, for various different reasons, the option of exile was chosen over execution, and so it was that Lazarus, as well as his sister Martha and another sister called Mary, also known as the Magdalene, set sail across the Mediterranean Sea and arrived on the southeastern coast of the region that is today called France.

The oral tradition that has been handed down from one generation to the next gives us the following names of those who were in that fateful boat, which was to make of France "the Eldest Daughter of the Church": Mary Magdalene, Martha, Lazarus, Maximin, Mary Jacobe, Salome,

Marcelle, Cedonius and Sara. Interestingly, at least two of these people were witnesses of the Crucifixion of Christ and also saw him after his glorious Resurrection. They were consequently Christians of the most convinced and zealous kind, and soon their zeal would lead to numerous souls being led to the saving fonts of Baptism.

Saint Mary Magdalene no doubt spoke to all she met about the Risen Lord's apparitions to her, and in this way the Catholic and apostolic Faith planted the deepest roots in the fertile soil of Gaul. The grace bequeathed to this privileged people has never failed to produce the most magnificent examples of holiness throughout the history of the Church. It is as though the love with which Christ loved the family of Bethany has somehow been shared with the people of France; they have received an unending stream of private revelations of that love. Saint Mary Magdalene participated in this initial evangelisation of Provence, but eventually her choice of the "better part", that is to say, her desire to fix the gaze of her contemplative heart on the holy face of Jesus in an uninterrupted manner, overpowered her soul; and this time the contemplative vocation was never to be "taken from her" again. She found what is perhaps one of the most perfect locations in the entire region for a life of peace and solitude, in a grotto halfway up the mountain of la Sainte Baume, and there she lived out the final years of her mortal life.

It is hard to describe the enchanting beauty of the location that became her final dwelling place on earth and where it seems as though the peace of eternity has spilled over into the universe. Perhaps it would be best to invoke the aid of a master of language whose eloquence did so much to rebuild the Church in France upon the ruins left by the terror of the Revolution. He is credited not only with bringing the Dominican Order back to France after its total eradication, but also with bringing devotion back to la Sainte Baume. His words, though removed from the richness of their original language, still give us a hint of how Father Henri Lacordaire felt as he trekked through the forests of la Sainte Baume before finally catching a glimpse of the old abandoned Dominican convent adjacent to the holy grotto, where the wonders of mystical grace had borne much fruit:

> In the midst of these rows of elevated rocks, which resemble a stone curtain, the eye picks out a dwelling which seems as if suspended in the air, and at its feet a forest whose novelty is striking. It is no longer the thin and fragrant pine of Provence, nor the green oak, nor anything of the shadowy coverings the traveler has come across on his journey; one would say that by some inexplicable prodigy the North had flung down in that spot all the magnificence of its vegetation. It is the sun and the sky of the South with the planted woods of England. Close by, only a few feet away, on the side of the mountain, one finds once again the true nature of the country; this particular spot is the one exception. And if one penetrates the forest, it immediately covers you with all its majesty, similar in its depths, its veils and its silences, to those sacred woods which the axes of the Ancients would never profane. There also only the centuries have access; they alone have exercised the right to cut down the old trunks and to renew their sap; only they have reigned and reign yet, instruments of a respect which comes from something higher than themselves, and which adds to the sudden emotion of sight, that of thought. Who then has

passed by here? Who has marked this corner of the earth with such a powerful imprint? What is this mass of rock? What is this forest? What is this place where everything seems greater than us? Oh Marseille! You witnessed the arrival of the guest who first inhabited this mountain. You saw alight from a bark the frail creature who brought you the second visit from the East. The first had given you your port, your walls, your name, your very existence; the second gave you something even better, it entrusted to you the living relics of the life of Jesus Christ, the souls which He had loved most tenderly on earth, and, so to speak, the supreme testament of the friendship of a God. It was from the summit of His cross that Jesus Christ had bequeathed His mother to John the Apostle; for you, it was from the summit of His resurrection, between those shadows, which had been drawn aside, of death and the white light of eternal life that Jesus chose you to be the tested refuge of his dearest friends.[1]

Surrounded by the perfect stillness of the place, which no pilgrim fails to comment upon, Mary's every breath became a silent prayer of love, and very often she would experience moments of supernatural ecstasy, true fore-tastes of the delights of the heavenly Jerusalem.

Saint Maximin, who had become a father to the Christians of the surrounding region, spent much time in a little village that Mary could just about glimpse from the entrance of her grotto and through which passed the great Roman road known as the Via Aurelia. So important was this man of God in the memory of the locals that one day their village would be renamed after him.

[1] Henri Lacordaire, *Marie-Madeleine* (Paris: Éditions du Cerf, 2009), pp. 16–17.

Saint Maximin made sure that the saintly woman he was privileged to have accompanied from the Holy Land was regularly nourished with the Bread of Life. Blessed Anne Catherine Emmerich presents us with the memorable image of Magdalene descending from the grotto through the lush green forest of Sainte Baume to meet Saint Maximin halfway when he brought her the gift of Holy Communion.[2] Her life of prayer and love for the Eucharist must have grown to ever new levels of intensity, for the local tradition has it that Magdalene eventually partook of no other food but this heavenly Manna and left this world in a eucharistic ecstasy after receiving Holy Communion for the last time. She, who clung to the feet of her Lord in loving adoration during his mortal life, clung to him so tightly when he came in the Eucharist that for her it became the beginning of the mystical marriage of Paradise. Such were the marvels that la Sainte Baume was privileged to behold almost two thousand years ago. To understand Mary Magdalene, however, we must go even farther back in time and return to the sunny days in Galilee when her soul first passed from death to life.

[2] Anne Catherine Emmerich, *Visions d'Anne Catherine Emmerich*, volume 3, translated by Charles d'Eberling (Paris: Téqui, 1995), p. 417.

I

One Woman or Three?

Before we immerse ourselves in a meditation of the scriptural texts that will teach us many secrets about the interior journey to holiness of Saint Mary Magdalene, it is first necessary to mention the contemporary controversy surrounding her identity; and in order to do this, we will also be obliged to discuss some questions of an exegetical nature. The goal of this first part of the book will be to show the reasonableness of continuing to believe the traditional portrait of the saint that the Church of ancient times painted for her children. Since the identity of Saint Mary Magdalene is today somewhat of an open question, and since the Church has left us the freedom to reflect upon and debate it, we must also affirm that the faithful are free to reject the traditional image we will present. The Church herself has no official position on this question, and even in her modern liturgy she no longer explicitly associates Saint Mary Magdalene with the repentant sinner of the Gospel of Luke. In recent years there has been too much debate among the greatest of biblical scholars for the Church to propose as certain what is so seriously contested.

So how did we Catholics arrive at the situation we know

today, whereby the identity of Saint Mary Magdalene is hotly debated and often confused? In the early Church there was also a certain amount of disagreement about her identity, but in the Western Church, the Fathers managed to agree upon a particular vision of the saint that was more or less unanimously accepted until the early twentieth century. The main crux of the debated question can be summarised as follows: Is Mary Magdalene, from whom went forth seven demons and who was witness to the Resurrection, one and the same as the sinful woman who was converted to Christ in the seventh chapter of the Gospel of Luke? And is she also the person who is described as the sister of Lazarus and Martha, whom we read so much about in the Gospel of John? Many today would simply respond no, while at the same time not really being able to explain why they are so certain that this is the case. If they jogged their memory a little they would probably recall that a priest once preached this to them, and if we were to go back and ask the priest in question to jog his memory, he would probably say that he vaguely recalls some professor in seminary telling him that this was the case. As we said above, however, in the not so distant past, the answer of the Roman Catholic Church to this question was an emphatic yes.

In the first centuries of Christianity some Eastern Fathers adopted the position that Mary Magdalene, Mary the sister of Martha, and the sinful woman who washes the feet of Jesus with her tears of remorse were three different women, and this position later went on to become that of the Eastern Orthodox Church. The Western Fathers disagreed, however, and the authority of intellectual giants such as Saint Augustine and Pope Saint Gregory the Great was sufficient to convince the entire Catholic Church that the relevant Scripture passages were not speaking of three different women but only one.[1] Raban Maur, in his ninth-century work on the life of Saint Mary Magdalene, building upon books from earlier centuries, confirmed the universal acceptance of this understanding of her identity—not only her identity but also her exile to Gaul was well known to all of Christendom. Devotion to Saint Mary Magdalene, the model of penitents, flourished everywhere, and the Basilica of Saint Maximin eventually became known as the Third Tomb of Christendom.

This position was not called into question in the West until the sixteenth century, when Protestant authors began to reject many Catholic traditions. Their works soon began to influence certain Catholics too. The sixteenth-century philologist Lefèvre d'Etaples published a work rejecting this tradition. He was followed by the Spanish scholar Balthazar Socco, but the great Saint John Fisher of England refuted their ideas. Fisher was backed up by Saint Thomas More, who was deeply devoted to the traditional image of Saint Mary Magdalene. More understood the importance of retaining a clear picture of a saint who had displayed so much love for Christ in the Gospels.[2] Eventually the position of d'Etaples and Socco was officially

---

[1] An explanation of the changes and developments in Saint Augustine's position on this question is provided by J. P. Ravotti in his book entitled *Sainte Marie-Madeleine—Evangiles et Traditions* (Geménos: Horizons Publishing, 2010), pp. 43–67.

[2] James Monti, *The King's Good Servant but God's First* (San Francisco: Ignatius Press, 1997), p. 88.

condemned by the authoritative theological faculty of the Sorbonne.

In the subsequent centuries, Protestant communities continued to move further away from the ancient tradition, but Catholics became more and more convinced, thanks in part to the influence of the writings of the French school of spirituality. The private revelations of mystics who claimed to have had visions of the life of Christ in which penitent Magdalene was indeed the sister of Lazarus also strongly reinforced the traditional image of the saint in the minds of the Catholic faithful. Popular Catholic mystics Mary of Agreda, Anne Catherine Emmerich and Maria Valtorta confirmed not only the traditional identification of Mary Magdalene but also the ages-old belief that she ended her days in a grotto in Gaul. For the average Catholic there was no question or debate about the identity of Mary Magdalene. For centuries the Tridentine liturgy proclaimed it. It was only through the biblical scholarship of the twentieth century that opposition to this position resurfaced.

So how exactly did we go from unanimously teaching that Mary Magdalene was the sister of Lazarus and a repentant sinner to an almost unanimous rejection of this teaching, especially in the English-speaking world? The answer is simply that the writings of several influential exegetes convinced most university professors to reject the traditional belief; they in turn formed the bishops and the priests of the second half of the twentieth century, who influenced the understanding of the faithful. For the most part this radical shift in our way of understanding such an extraordinarily important saint has trickled down from the pages of biblical exegesis to the average Catholic in the pew in a remarkably short period of time and often with very little resistance along the way.

In the latter part of the twentieth century there was another contributing factor. A feminist and largely North American current of thought that entered into Catholic scholarship reinterpreted Mary Magdalene's ancient title "Apostle to the Apostles". This title was fittingly assigned to Mary because in the Gospels she is the first to see the Risen Lord, who asks her to tell the apostles about his Resurrection. Some feminists, however, used the title to propose the saint as a patron for the cause of female ordination. As scholars began to recreate Magdalene's personality to match an ideological objective with respect to the priesthood, they began to reject certain aspects of the traditional belief. The idea of Mary once being a public sinner with a tainted reputation and then later becoming a deeply contemplative soul, inclined more to silence than to making herself heard in the crowd, did not fit with the vision of her being a liberated woman, in the modern sense of the word, involved in power struggles with the apostles. Through writing, teaching and lecturing some feminist scholars countered the Church's veneration of Mary as the model of penitents and contemplatives.

The rejection of the traditional Mary Magdalene is widespread in Anglo-Saxon biblical thought; the same cannot be said, however, for exegesis in France, and this is largely due to the influence of one man: Father André Feuillet (1909–1998). Feuillet, without doubt one of the greatest French exegetes of the twentieth century, is unfortunately not well known in the English-speaking academic world although more and more people are beginning to ask questions about his work, especially since he was quoted several times in the book *Jesus of Nazareth* by Pope Benedict XVI, upon whom he has had much influence. Students of Professor Scott Hahn will also be aware of Feuillet, for he has helped to shape some of his interpretations of the Gospel of John. Unlike many of his contemporaries, Feuillet remained firmly convinced that the Church had correctly interpreted the texts traditionally associated with Saint Mary Magdalene.[3]

In the following chapters we will devote ourselves to a meditative commentary of the scriptural texts that have always been associated with Saint Mary Magdalene, but first it will be a useful exercise to summarise the exegetical position of André Feuillet. This section of the book will perhaps be more technical than what follows, but the exegetical questions will be discussed as succinctly as possible and will help us to see that the teaching of the ancient Church was not as unfounded as some modern scholars would have us believe. With the validity or at least the coherence of the traditional position established, we will then be in a position to paint a portrait of Saint Mary Magdalene as one who traces out an itinerary of holiness through which the greatest of sinners among us can dare to hope to become the greatest of saints.

---

[3] For an analysis of the identity question see André Feuillet, "Les Deux Onctions Faites sur Jésus, et Marie-Madeleine", *Revue Thomiste*, LXXV, 1975, pp. 358–94.

A tale of two anointings

The first problem we encounter is that the Gospels are not explicit in identifying the woman who is first called a sinner, secondly the sister of Martha and thirdly Mary Magdalene. We will call the idea that these three women are really one and the same woman the "identification theory". The fact that the Gospels do not explicitly explain this identification, however, is not by itself a sufficient reason for dismissing it as untrue. Scripture is often mysteriously vague, or rather, difficult to interpret, sometimes even in relation to some of the most important realities in the life of the Church. The controversies surrounding the interpretation of texts that speak of the Eucharist, the privileges of the Blessed Virgin Mary and the transmission of the charism of Peter show us that deep meditation and the help of the Church are often absolutely necessary if we are to understand what the Holy Spirit wants to teach us in Scripture. A surface reading can often lead to grave misunderstanding of essential truths of faith because Scripture is by nature a mystery that demands humble and prayerful meditation. In addition, the Gospels were not written in the same way as modern works that seek to argue their points by appealing to historical proofs, providing exact times, dates, names, places etc. The sacred authors lived in an entirely different cultural context with very different levels of education, and they were intent above all upon simply presenting the beauty of the Person of Jesus Christ, as well as whatever we need to know to be able to believe in him and be saved (see Jn 20:31). As one scholar has put it: "Evangelists are not journalists!" If they were writing a historical work according to modern standards they would set the scene by giving us the full background of all major characters. For example, they would give us many personal details about Lazarus, whom we first encounter in the Gospels on his deathbed. They would explain his family origins, where he was born and studied, what he did for a living, his marital situation, who would inherit his fortune, the type of sickness he had and for how long it had been bothering him. Instead they basically just tell us that he had two sisters, he was dying and Jesus loved him. Enough said for an evangelist!

Feuillet begins his commentary by lamenting the fact that certain contemporary scholars use biblical criticism to create more problems than they solve.[4] Alas, he says, we often use it to demolish rather than to construct, and it has been used by some scholars to sow so much confusion about Saint Mary Magdalene that today Christians do not know what to think or say about her anymore. Some will not tolerate any mention of the identification theory, which was universally accepted only a few decades ago. Thus we are tempted to neglect any kind of in-depth or coherent commentary upon the texts that have always been associated with her and, according to Marie-Joseph Lagrange, are among the most touching in Scripture. The different theories on these texts, moreover, are so contradictory and lacking in unanimity that very often all they leave us with is uncertainty.[5]

---

[4] See A. Feuillet, p. 358.
[5] Ibid., p. 362.

The major exegetical debate revolves around the interpretation of the two different anointings of Jesus Christ, the first of which takes place in Luke 7:36–50, in the early days of Christ's public ministry in Galilee. The second anointing, which resembles the first, takes place a few days before Christ's death in the village of Bethany, which lies a couple of miles from Jerusalem (see Jn 12:1–8; Mt 26:6–13; Mk 14:3–9). Feuillet, writing in the year 1975, begins his analysis of these texts with a brief summary of some of the modern positions, which through their interpretation of these two anointings have led to the deconstruction of the traditional identity of the saint. He begins with a short word on the thought of Rudolf Bultmann, who basically suggests that these texts were not historical but literary insertions to highlight the practical application of certain teachings of Christ on key themes. In other words, the events in question would be a kind of "clothing" provided to adorn the body of these important doctrines of Christ. Feuillet then turns his thoughts to the Catholic scholars who have played the most important role in shaping modern exegesis of these texts. For anyone who seriously reflects upon the subject, it seems unlikely that two different women would have performed such a unique and downright strange act as the anointing of Christ's feet. Faced with this problem, the Catholic exegetes had to adopt a different strategy in order to explain the two anointings. In 1954 André Légault published a work in which he suggests that the two anointings were really just one anointing and their separation was a result of some confusion in the way the oral tradition was handed down to the sacred authors.

This idea was then taken up by Rudolf Schnackenburg and above all by Raymond Brown. In his reflections upon this issue Brown eventually adopts the idea that both texts speak of a single event, an anointing of Christ's feet carried out at some point by an anonymous woman. He does so, however, with certain reservations and he points out several problems with this interpretation. The most notable question he raises is about the identity of Mary of Bethany. If she did not anoint Christ's feet then how can we explain the fact that in the early Johannine community she seems to have been known as "Mary who anointed the Lord with ointment and wiped his feet with her hair" (Jn 11:2)? This important question he eventually brushes aside so as to move on to other considerations.

Another author, J. K. Elliott, similarly suggests that there was only one anointing event and that each evangelist explained it in his own way in accordance with the principal substance of his own particular message. For example Luke, always intent upon highlighting the mercy of Christ, used the episode to explain the forgiveness of a sinner.[6] There have certainly been other perhaps more interesting and at times more convoluted positions adopted since the time Feuillet wrote on this subject, but it is clear from the brief glance at twentieth-century exegesis provided by him that this question lacks clarity. Scholars are often unable to arrive at a logical conclusion without first doing some injury to the integrity of the texts and at times the inerrancy of Scripture itself. I

[6] Ibid., pp. 364–66

would thus like to move rapidly on to the interpretation of the texts provided by Feuillet himself, since he manages to respect the integrity of the inspired Word and also arrive at a perfectly reasonable identification of this mysterious woman. Feuillet begins with a comparison of the two anointings. The first is described only in Luke 7:36–50, while the second anointing is recounted by Matthew, Mark and John (Mt 26:6–13; Mk 14:3–9; Jn 12:1–8). The first stumbling block we encounter when comparing the texts is the fact that in relation to the second anointing, Mark and Matthew tell us that the perfumed oil was applied to the head of Christ, while John explains that it was applied to Christ's feet. Feuillet proposes a very commonsense solution to this problem. Most scholars agree that John is often providing information that was not provided by the other evangelists, who wrote their Gospels before he did and which were well known at the time of his writing. He often fills in the gaps, so to speak, and at times he seems to presuppose the reader's knowledge of the synoptic tradition. John never denies what has been written by other evangelists, but he relies quite freely on his own unique memory of events and adds new details he considers important. As an eyewitness to the second anointing, he adds the startling detail that was not recorded by the other Gospels, namely, that the oil was applied to the feet of Christ.

Saint Augustine says that the anointing of the feet happened immediately after that of the head. Marie-Joseph Lagrange, the founder of the École Biblique in Jerusalem, puts it this way: "Mary anointed the head of Jesus following the usual custom, then as there still remained much perfume, she put it on his feet."[7] Feuillet explains that this interpretation is not contrived but perhaps the only one possible, in light of the words of Christ in relation to this gesture. It was a very normal custom to anoint the head of a respected guest, and in the Gospel of Luke Jesus makes clear that he has been slighted by the Pharisee who did not perform this simple gesture of respect for him (7:44–46). If Mary had done no more than anoint his head, then Jesus would hardly have praised her action as worthy of eternal memory, nor would he have said that it was his "body" that had been anointed. The anointing of his head would have been an ordinary occurrence, while the anointing of his feet was worthy of special note.

Feuillet turns back to the earlier anointing described by Luke alone and immediately rejects the idea that it is the same event. It happens in a completely different location and at a completely different moment in the life of Christ. It has a completely different context and meaning, as this first anointing is characterised by the repentant tears of a sinful woman, whereas in the second anointing there is no mention of tears but a reference to the poor and the impending burial of the Lord. In the first case, Christ's head is not anointed but only his feet. Here there is no sign of the service of Martha, who would have ensured that Christ would have received every necessary sign of hospitality. The perfume used seems to be of inferior quality to that in the second anointing, for its use provokes no outrage on the part of the witnesses.

[7] M.J. Lagrange, *L'Évangile selon saint Jean* (Paris: Victor Lecoffre, 1925), p. 323.

There is one noticeable similarity in that the first and the second hosts are both called Simon. However this similarity is no grounds for artificially fusing the two events. If we consider the apostolic group alone, the common name of Simon is found twice among the Twelve. If one-sixth of the apostles happen to be called Simon, we should not be surprised if the name is found elsewhere. The man called Simon in the first anointing is a Pharisee, and the fact that he invites Jesus to a meal is not surprising, as at that time the pharisaical animosity directed towards the Lord was less intense; but by the time of the second anointing, most of the Pharisees had firmly rejected Christ and were actively persecuting those who put their faith in him (Jn 11:45-54). The Simon in the second anointing is not a Galilean Pharisee but is called the "leper" and seems to be a friend of Christ from Bethany. He is most likely a leper who had been healed by Jesus and who had befriended him as a result.[8] A healthy respect for the accuracy of the Gospel narratives should make us conclude that we are talking about two different events, involving two different audiences, taking place in two very different places and times.

The main problem for exegetes in accepting these as two separate events is that the activity of the women doing the anointing is so similar that we are tempted to doubt there could have been two events in the public life of Christ that resemble each other so closely. We would like to resolve the whole problem in a convenient way by merging them into one single event. As mentioned above,

---

[8] Feuillet, A., pp. 369-70.

however, the two anointings, while being alike in some ways, have some important differences; thus we cannot lump them together without first doing damage to the integrity of Scripture. The doubts about the authenticity of the two anointings and the exegetical temptation to suggest that both refer to the same event can all be resolved, according to Feuillet, by concluding that there were two different anointings carried out by the same woman. The similarities, then, come not from the text and its context but rather from the personality and the gestures of this mysterious woman who comes bearing her alabaster jar of perfume. As the great French Dominican preacher Henri Lacordaire once put it, there were two anointings carried out by one soul, two different anointings indeed but one heart conceived them both. "There are things that can be repeated by the soul that conceived them, but which can never be initiated by another."[9]

The more time we spend meditating on the second anointing, the more we are puzzled as to how anybody could doubt that this is the same woman who first anointed Christ in Galilee and who went so far as to dry his feet with her hair. This is no ordinary behavior. Is it really likely that two different women did such an unusual thing? This unique pattern in the activity of a single figure recurring more than once explains why both anointings are so similar and yet clearly different. Only this conclusion allows us to hold the differences and similarities in a perfect balance. In the end we seem to be left with only

[9] Henri Lacordaire, *Marie-Madeleine* (Paris: Éditions du Cerf, 2009), p. 41.

one of two choices: either we say that there was only one anointing and then we call into question the accuracy of Scripture itself, or we say that there is a single personality shining through the woman in both texts, a single personality that is at two very different stages in her relationship with Jesus. By the time of the second anointing there is no more need for tears of repentance, for she is by now a dear friend of Christ and a true saint in the making. She is repeating the gesture of the early days of her conversion and it has become something of her own personal devotion to Christ. That we are talking about one and the same person in both texts was the conclusion of Saint Augustine and the entire Western tradition after him until the twentieth century. In the 1930s, as the first doubts about this teaching began to appear in the Church, the great Jesuit author Alban Goodier wrote the following in his commentary on the holy women we encounter in chapter 8 of the Gospel of Luke:

> Who was Mary Magdalene? This is no place for controversy; we are painting a picture and no more. We will only say here that we are unconvinced by all the arguments which seek to destroy the popular tradition of the Church. Their strength lies in ignoring the singular consistency of character and action, the singular sameness of devotion and demonstration and almost reckless love which marks one woman from the day we meet her at the feet of Jesus in Magdala to the day we leave her at the same feet after the Resurrection. The letter may be turned against her, the spirit of the Gospel story seems to read entirely in her favour; and Saint Luke who characteristically in the scene of her humiliation declines to give her name, calls her only "a woman of the city, who was

a sinner'', now immediately after, when she is installed as the leader of the penitent women who followed Jesus and served him, delights to give her her full title, Mary Magdalene.[10]

A Johannine clarification reinforces the argument

There is one other detail given by Saint John, which compels us to conclude that the first anointing was carried out by the woman who performed the second one, that is, by the sister of Lazarus whom we sometimes call Mary of Bethany. The second anointing takes place in chapter 12 of the Gospel of John, but if we turn back to the beginning of chapter 11 of that Gospel we find the following interesting statement: "It was Mary who anointed the Lord with ointment and wiped his feet with her hair, whose brother Lazarus was ill'' (11:2). If there were two different women who had accomplished such a gesture it would be useless to characterise Mary of Bethany as *the* woman who did this. Something else in this text, however, is even more important: John tells us that Mary did this in the past. He uses the verb for "anointed" in the aorist tense and is definitely referring to a past event. He makes this reference a chapter in advance, that is, several weeks before, the anointing in Bethany. If he had been speaking of the future anointing he would have put the verb in the future tense as he does when he explains that Judas "was to betray" Jesus at a later moment (Jn 6:71).[11]

[10] Alban Goodier, S.J., *The Public Life of Our Lord Jesus Christ*, volume I (New York: P.J. Kenedy and Sons, 1931), p. 276.

[11] Ibid., p. 372.

Some insist that regardless of the grammatical anomaly, John is in fact anticipating the future anointing, but only rarely does an author speak about something that will occur later in his story. John does this in the case of Judas to make clearer the words of Jesus, who knows in advance that Judas will betray him, and to alert those who might already know the story of the betrayal. In the case of Mary of Bethany, John seems to be aware that the story of the first anointing, as told by Luke, was already known by his audience. What they perhaps did not know is the identity of that unnamed woman, which John takes the opportunity to reveal. This statement of John is a thorn in the side for those who oppose the identification theory, and for Feuillet it is a statement that many have failed to consider adequately.[12] Although he was no great defender of Catholic tradition, the Anglican scholar J. H. Bernard felt compelled to admit that John was identifying Mary of Bethany with the sinful woman of Luke 7. He called this an inevitable conclusion, for "Christian readers of the next generation would not be helped by an explanatory note which might equally be applied to two distinct women."[13]

The woman who does something beautiful

Another question that Feuillet addresses is why Mary, whose brother and sister live in Bethany, might also be called Mary Magdalene or literally Mary the Magdalene,

[12] Ibid.

[13] J. H. Bernard, *The International Critical Commentary on the Gospel of John* (Edinburgh: T&T Clark, 1928), p. 373.

a title which identifies her with the town of Magdala. This identification does not automatically mean she was born there but may simply denote that she lived there for some time. (I was born in England and spent much of my childhood there, but because I have lived a long time in Ireland, I am almost always described as an Irish priest.) When reading the Gospels it is striking to note how few of Christ's close disciples are identified with a town. We do not call Andrew the "Bethsaidian" nor Matthew the "Capernaumian". If at times a man is identified with a town (Nathaniel of Cana), it is highly unusual for a woman to be identified in this way. It is common for a woman to be associated with her husband and her family, and much less common for her to be associated with a place. To call Mary the Magdalene is unusual and is perhaps connected to a reputation that she may have won for herself in the town of Magdala.

The ancient Provençal tradition has always held that Mary Magdalene was from a wealthy family who lived in Bethany but at a certain moment she went to live in the town of Magdala, situated on the picturesque shores of the Sea of Galilee and populated by a high number of pagan inhabitants. The influx of the heathen had scandalised the local Jews because it lowered the moral standards of the place. Here, in this seductive environment, Mary was led away from her childhood fidelity to the Law of Moses; then to the shame of her respected family in Bethany, she fell so far that she became known by the Jews as a public sinner, the notorious Magdalene. She was converted upon encountering Christ in the early days of his public ministry and eventually we find her, at a much later date, back in Bethany, spending time with her family once again. Even though this family lived in Judaea, a long way from where Christ grew up and spent most of his public ministry, this family seems to be particularly close to Jesus in the Gospel of John. Such a relationship would be explained by the fact that Magdalene got to know Christ in Galilee and that thanks to her conversion Jesus became the object of the most sincere affection on the part of her family. Our Lord spent prolonged periods of time working in Galilee and in Perea, but the Gospels show that he did not spend all that much time in Judaea. Whenever he would visit, he could always count on the grateful family of Bethany to make him feel at home.

From the Gospels we learn a few important details about Mary Magdalene. She is a woman described as being exorcised or liberated by Jesus from "seven demons", but this liberation is not clearly explained. After her liberation she becomes a member of the community of disciples and especially the women who contribute generously to help Jesus and the apostles with their material needs. Twice she is found on a list of names next to Joanna, the wife of Herod's steward, an extremely influential man called Chuza, and so she may have been associated with King Herod's court before her conversion. Her name does not appear very often during the public ministry of Jesus, but she is definitely present at the side of the Blessed Virgin Mary at the foot of the Cross. Perhaps most exceptional is the fact that she is present at the empty tomb on Easter Sunday morning, when the Risen Lord chooses to appear to her before his own apostles and to give her the mission of proclaiming the truth of his Resurrection for the first time in human history. She must truly be a dear friend of Christ in order to have received such privileges.

Apart from the fact that her first name is also Mary, can she be reconciled to the image of Mary of Bethany as explained above? The fact that she was the one from whom went forth seven demons, somewhere in Galilee, would correspond to the identity of the sinful woman converted in tears at the feet of Jesus, and so this part of her identity would easily match up with that of a repentant sinner; but it is helpful to look more deeply at some of the key texts in order to identify other possible connections.

After years of studying this question Feuillet was firmly convinced that Mary Magdalene is merely another title for Mary the sister of Lazarus, whom today we like to call Mary of Bethany. He nonetheless admits that this identification is not immediately evident but rests upon what he calls a convergence of probabilities. This kind of argument is often used when studying historical events and seeking to make certain conclusions for which the proofs are not all fully available. Basically what we mean by this is that by observing the details available we can draw the most probable conclusion. He believes that the tradition the Western Church agreed upon in relation to Saint Mary Magdalene was in fact the most probable conclusion based upon the available facts. Some will be surprised by Feuillet's conclusion that the identification theory is more probable than the theory that there were three different women.

Perhaps the most important argument employed by

Feuillet is the one also employed by Saint Thomas Aquinas in his commentary on chapter 12 of the Gospel of John. (Aquinas presents both the Eastern and the Western opinions, but seems to accept and build upon the position of the West.) We can summarise the Western position as follows: Mary of Bethany is praised by Jesus for anointing his body for burial. She is close enough to Christ to be the one chosen by heaven to accomplish this all important work of love. It is therefore reasonable to expect to find this same woman present on Easter Sunday morning with the other holy women who go to anoint Christ's body, since they had been prevented from doing so properly before the tomb was quickly closed before the Sabbath.

One thing is certain, she is a woman associated with anointing his body for burial and the first person to try to do that is a woman called Mary Magdalene. Saint Thomas Aquinas wrote the following:

> He adds, let her keep it for the day of my burial, foretelling both his approaching death and the kindness this woman was ready to do for him in his tomb if he had not precluded it by rising so soon, for as we read in Mark's Gospel (16:1): "Mary Magdalene," along with other women, "bought spices, so that they might go and anoint him." This is why he said, let her keep it for the day of my burial, not the identical ointment she used, but ointment of the same kind, in general or particular, or even a similar service. It is as though he were saying: Do not stop her from doing for me while I am alive what she will be unable to do for me when I am dead. For, as I said, she was prevented by the resurrection of Christ occurring so quickly. This is expressed in a clearer way

in Mark (14:8): "She has anointed my body beforehand for burying."[14]

Feuillet goes further than the Angelic Doctor. He notices that among the women present at the time of the Passion and the Resurrection there are three called Mary: Mary the Mother of God; her sister Mary, the wife of Clopas and the mother of James the Lesser; and Mary Magdalene. We know something about the identity of the first two women, and in light of their kinship to Christ, their presence on Calvary does not surprise us; but we know very little about Mary Magdalene if she is not Mary of Bethany. Is it probable that she, who if not Mary of Bethany scarcely appears on the pages of the Gospels during the public life of Christ, would not only be present at the Cross but would also receive such a privileged apparition at the Resurrection?

It seems more probable that Mary Magdalene is Mary of Bethany, the sister of Lazarus, who would otherwise not be mentioned in the texts relating the Passion and Resurrection, in spite of her closeness to Christ and her association with anointing him for burial. Her anointing expressed the purest love for Christ, and it would take more than the Passion to separate such a loving soul from her Lord. In fact, the sufferings of Christ would only serve to draw the greatest compassion out of a soul who knows so much about love. It may be that she receives her apparition of the Risen Lord as a kind of acknowledgement of the "beautiful thing" she did for Jesus in anointing him for burial (Mt 26:10). It is Jesus him-

[14] Thomas Aquinas, *Commentary on John*, n. 1608.

self who proclaims that this woman has begun his funeral ritual. It seems logical that on Easter Sunday, Mary of Bethany, which incidentally is a name that Scripture never uses, comes back to finish that ritual. Frank Sheed summed it up well: "It is hard to believe that the Mary who was absorbed in contemplation of him in Bethany did not travel the two miles to be with him on Calvary. It is hard, too, to believe that the Mary who anointed his feet in Simon's house—'for my burial' our Lord said (Mt 26:12)—would not have been of the party that brought sweet spices to anoint Jesus in the tomb."[15]

Feuillet encourages deep meditation on the texts in order to grasp this mystery. When Mary the sister of Lazarus anointed the feet of Jesus with costly ointment in Bethany, Jesus said something very unusual when Judas asked why the ointment was not sold and the money given to the poor: "Let her keep it for the day of my burial" (Jn 12:7). Our Lord often says things in a manner that is at first incomprehensible so that his listeners will meditate on his words more deeply. The word Jesus uses for "burial" in the Greek text refers more specifically to the ritual of embalming. Christ is therefore suggesting that he will die very soon and that Mary has begun his burial rites. Mary probably did not understand what Jesus was saying but was simply following the inspirations of love in her heart when she anointed him. Given that Jesus chose her to anoint his body, however, it is almost impossible to imagine that she would not go to the tomb on Easter

---

[15] Frank Sheed, *To Know Christ Jesus* (San Francisco: Ignatius Press, 1992), p. 285.

Sunday to finish the rite she had begun. If we do not identify Mary of Bethany with Mary Magdalene, then she is not at the tomb.

At the anointing in Bethany Jesus said that the praiseworthy memory of what Mary did for him would be recounted wherever the gospel is preached (cf. Mt 26:13). Yet who has ever heard a preacher sing the praises of Saint Mary of Bethany or the Church invoke her intercession in her litanies? If she is Saint Mary Magdalene, however, then Christ's prophecy has been fulfilled in every generation. There is no feast day for an individual called Mary of Bethany, but the feast day of Saint Martha of Bethany takes place on the octave day of the feast of Saint Mary Magdalene.

There are still other convergences of probability that link the two Marys in these texts. When Mary of Bethany anointed Jesus with her costly perfume, Judas, as we have seen, cried out that it should have been sold and the money given to the poor. He said this not because "he cared for the poor but because he was a thief, and as he had the money box he used to take what was put into it" (Jn 12:6). When we read this in light of the fact that Luke put the name of Mary Magdalene on the list of women who contributed to the material needs of the apostolic group with her own goods, we can understand why Judas knew that if the perfume had been sold, the money would most certainly have come to him as treasurer of the apostolic funds.[16]

To conclude, Feuillet provides another interesting idea,

[16] Feuillet, p. 377.

taken this time from the liturgy of the Church, through which the Holy Spirit often gives us light to understand deep mysteries in Scripture. For the feast of Saint Mary Magdalene the Church gives us the Gospel taken from John 20 in which Mary is weeping and seeking her beloved Jesus everywhere. The first reading for that feast is a prefiguration of this text found in the third chapter of the Song of Songs. It speaks of a woman desperately longing to see her Beloved, running through the streets and then asking people where he is gone. The Church wants us to see in Mary Magdalene this mystical spouse from the Song of Songs going through a kind of first "dark night of the soul" experience. Another reference in the Song of Songs, however, makes us think of Mary of Bethany's anointing of Christ the King before he enters the kingly city of Jerusalem: "While the king was on his couch, my nard gave forth its fragrance" (Song 1:12). Only twice in Scripture is nard mentioned, first in the mystical dialogues of the Song of Songs and secondly when Mary of Bethany fills the house with its fragrance, as the king is at table, reclined on his couch. If the Church sends us back to a meditation on the Song of Songs and there shows us a woman who is at one moment a prefiguration of the one we call Saint Mary Magdalene and at another a prefiguration of Mary of Bethany, we can understand why this saint has been referred to by one French preacher as "the woman cut in pieces".

The identification of Mary of Bethany with Mary Magdalene is the conclusion drawn by many doctors and saints throughout the history of the Church, and it is not only a perfectly reasonable conclusion but Feuillet would add that it is the most probable one. We will return briefly to certain exegetical questions throughout the course of these meditations, but for now we have said enough to begin to sketch the identity of the model of penitents and converts to Christ. As mentioned above, nobody is obliged to accept or reject this vision of Saint Mary Magdalene; the Church leaves us free to follow our hearts and to decide accordingly. The author is convinced that the ancient tradition of the Roman Catholic Church was correct, and if he is wrong he is happy to be wrong with those bright lights of Christian truth, namely, Saints Gregory, Augustine and Thomas Aquinas. These saintly masters of the spiritual interpretation of Scripture have opened up for us the meditation of one of the greatest conversion stories ever told, and the rest of this book will be a contemplative gaze at the encounters between this beautiful soul and the Lord Jesus Christ, the same Lord we encounter today in the mystery of the Most Holy Eucharist.

~

The Prodigal Daughter Comes Home

When first entering the Basilica of Saint Mary Magdalene in Provence one is immediately taken by the beauty of the ancient pulpit from which the great Dominicans of centuries gone by would preach their sermons on the patroness of their Order of Preachers, the one they love to call the Apostle to the Apostles. In the seven wooden engravings that surround the outside of the beautifully sculptured pulpit, we find an eighteenth-century artistic summary of the spiritual journey of the saint, from sinfulness to holiness. In gazing upon the first image on the pulpit, however, the visitor to the basilica is often unsure about which Gospel scene it refers to and rightly so. The truth is that it does not refer to any explicit Gospel scene. It depicts the Divine Lord seated in the authoritative posture of a teacher with his right hand raised, as though he is driving somebody out of his presence. Among his listeners there is a beautiful woman, dressed in a fine robe and extravagant jewelry. It is the old Mary, shortly before the moment of her radical conversion to Christ. The ancient tradition handed on in Saint Maximin, and especially in the last seven centuries by its Dominican preachers, is that Mary's first encounter with Christ is not recounted by the evangelists. She is said to have met Jesus somewhere in Galilee while he was preaching, and as would often occur when his all-powerful Word was pronounced, she was liberated from the evil that had bound her in its power. With his right hand raised in power, Christ is driving out of his presence the evil spirits that had made the life of this woman an unbearable nightmare.

We will see when we examine the Gospel texts more closely how they do seem to point us back to some first unrecorded encounter. We can imagine something of that moment of grace when Magdalene first felt called out of the darkness into God's wonderful light. It has been said that Saint Mary Magdalene was once a prostitute, but this is nowhere stated in the biblical texts that mention her. Since she seems to be a wealthy woman and a friend of the wife of Herod's steward, some have suggested that rather than being an ordinary prostitute she may have been a courtesan or some other kind of prominent member of the corrupt court of King Herod. He had attracted to the town of Tiberias a multitude of idolatrous pagans whose sinful behaviour spilled over into nearby Magdala and where many of them eventually settled down to live. History suggests that she would have had much contact with wickedness if indeed she had allowed herself to be seduced into company of the sort flanking the bloodthirsty king. Herod's court was the kind of place where one could witness the hunger for power bringing about the betrayal and the execution of innocent people. During the course of one particular festive meal the music came to a halt as the head of a holy man was carried into the banquet hall on a platter, merely because somebody's pride had been wounded by his words (Mt 14:1-12).

The exact nature of Mary's past life remains open to speculation, for all Scripture says about it is that she was known to be a sinful woman from whom seven demons went forth. Seven is the number that expresses completion or totality, and to speak of seven demons may suggest that she was afflicted by all kinds of sinful habits. She had done it all, so to speak. Demonic activity and sinful behaviour always go hand in hand, and the more the former is present the more disordered is the latter. Living in Magdala and coming into contact with so many pagans, Mary may also have participated in some of their rituals. For faithful Jews, this form of idolatry was the worst kind of sin one could commit. That alone would have been enough for the local Jews to refer to her with a sneer as "the Magdalene".

An ancient tradition says that Mary was of very wealthy stock and that her father was a man called Syrus, who owned property all over Israel. Upon the death of their father, her brother Lazarus remained in Jerusalem, while Bethany became the home of Martha, and Mary lived in a family property by the Sea of Galilee, in a coastal town called Magdala. She quickly became the subject of conversation in the town, for she was as beautiful as she was wealthy and such a combination often attracts the worst company. Amidst the wealthy foreigners who would flock to this area to partake in the pagan pastimes of nearby Tiberias, the Roman baths and the excitement of the hippodrome, Mary may have been seduced by the spirit of the world and tempted to live like the seemingly carefree pagans.[1]

In his book *Marie Madeleine* Raymond Bruckberger uses his great imagination and knowledge of ancient cultures to paint a fascinating picture of the personality of the saint before her conversion. At that time, Greek literature and philosophy, as well as the pagan practices of Roman culture, were held in great admiration by many worldly Jews who were growing tired of their own people's religiosity and much more pious way of life. The old temptation to become like the pagans had returned with force, especially now that Jews living in Alexandria and other great cites were coming back on pilgrimage to Jerusalem and recounting tales of what they were experiencing elsewhere. The Jews with a Greek education always seemed so much more cultivated than those of Judaea and so their example began to influence their brothers in the Holy Land.

A young wealthy woman like Magdalene may have received from her father a Greek education, but not being fervent enough in her faith and beset by the temptations of youth, she was enamoured of what she read of the free and exciting world of the Ancients. She would dream of being worshipped like some goddess of old. Like Cleopatra she too would use her beauty and wealth to have her own way and become somebody that this world would never forget. For Bruckberger, her decision to move to Magdala was partly motivated by the desire to break free from the moral shackles of Judaea and draw closer to

[1] Jean Gobi l'Ancien, *Miracles de Sainte Marie-Madeleine* (Paris: CNRS Éditions, 2009), p. 179.

the pagan liberty now emerging in the area surrounding Tiberias.[2]

The imagination of Bruckberger follows her as she first begins to go astray in Magdala and finally enters Herod's court, where she immediately becomes one of its most popular members. The immoral King Herod himself was mesmerised by the charms of this witty and strikingly beautiful young woman, whose free spirit made her the joy of his pagan guests. Men had always fallen at her feet, but now with the admiration of kings and princes adding fuel to the fire of her vanity, she was beginning to feel like Cleopatra. Amidst the company of such ruthless women as Herodias and her daughter, who had been made famous by her dancing, young Magdalene began to live the life she had dreamed of as an adolescent. After several years in this dark world of the rich and famous, however, she was left with nothing but a bitter heart and a troubled conscience. Every soul is made for infinite love, and when that love is sought outside of God, before long the soul finds itself in a state of sad frustration, especially when it has been created with a special capacity to love intensely. Magdalene began to grow sick of shallow, worldly conversations and longed for somebody to tell her the true meaning of her existence. She had also been deeply disturbed by all of the brutality she had witnessed. Nobody's life is safe where power and glory are prized so highly. How lovely would have been the liberating company of Christ the King after the oppressive company of Herod the tyrant.

[2] Raymond Léopold Bruckberger, O.P., *Marie Madeleine* (Paris: La Jeune Parque, 1953), p. 20.

In addition to the disgust she felt at what she had seen in royal circles, as well as the deep lack of fulfilment in her heart, Mary had another great problem about which she would rarely talk to anybody. Since her youth she had always felt a kind of interior darkness eating away at her heart, as though she had some kind of oppression of the soul, and at court she could feel that oppression growing heavier and heavier. She was tormented by nightmares and dark temptations of every kind, with thoughts too terrible to reveal. She would often experience overwhelming inclinations to evil and to self-annihilation, and of late this was beginning to frighten and disturb her all the more. The constant drunken celebrations with their false laughter were now becoming more and more unbearable for one who could no longer disguise that she was so deeply unhappy.

Bruckberger sees the arrival of Saint John the Baptist, and his holy presence and prayers in the dungeons of the palace, as providentially coinciding with the moment in which Magdalene eventually worked up the strength to break away from this den of vice. Not even the walls of his prison cell could stop the greatest of all the prophets from preparing hearts to meet the Christ. Since Scripture tells us that Herod liked to listen to the Baptist, it is possible that John would have had the chance to rebuke some poor sinners during the time he spent locked up in the palace. Perhaps Magdalene was among the very last of those hearts prepared by the Baptist to meet the Messiah.[3]

[3] Ibid., pp. 17–40.

With the same reckless freedom with which she had arrived, Mary now took her leave of Herod's palace, without even so much as a word about where she was going. The only person she would remain in contact with was Joanna, the wife of Chuza, who of late was also growing tired of the vanity of court life. Joanna would not be able to break free from the court of Herod so easily, and how she envied Magdalene, who told her that she had simply chosen to move on, to go elsewhere to continue her quest for the happiness she had always sought but was moving ever further from her grasp. There comes a moment of grace in every sinner's life, when he must make some choice upon which his salvation depends. At times it is something very simple, and perhaps in the case of Magdalene it was no more than the acceptance of an invitation to hear the new rabbi of whom all Galilee was talking. She was not in the habit of listening to preachers, but of late she had been experiencing such an inner torment from unsatisfied desire that she was ready to give anything a try.[4]

Also, with this dark pain within her soul she was beginning to think that she might perhaps be in need of some kind of spiritual healing. She was now at a crossroads and soon would have to choose between life and death. Mary Magdalene had reached the critical state that can lead to an awakening of the spirit and the discovery of true happiness, if only the person can humbly recognise his need for God and turn to him. As reluctant as she was to take this

[4] Pierre Sanson, *Marie Madeleine, Celle qui a beaucoup aimé* (Paris: Albin Michel, 1934), p. 62.

last step, she saw a glimmer of hope in what people were saying about the new rabbi who spoke of God in a new way and with such authority and eloquence. They said that his words were not like the lifeless and empty words of the Pharisees, whose dour sermons always brought a sense that the demands of the Law were beyond the reach of ordinary mortals. They said that his words were deep and beautiful, demanding, but always bringing hope and peace to those who heard them. So she decided to give him a chance.

Perhaps she made her way to the place where he was said to be preaching, upon some hilltop overlooking the lake and not far from the town of Capernaum, part of her felt a strange joy at the thought of what she was going to hear, but another part of her felt deep fear, almost panic, in the face of what was about to happen. In spite of the sudden temptations to flee and to stay away from this teacher, curiosity won out, and she forced herself to continue on her way towards the crowd that had gathered around the young rabbi dressed in white. As she came nearer the crowd she felt an irresistible force pulling her towards this mysterious man. She made her way forwards through the crowds, noticing that some people were clearly uncomfortable on seeing such a woman there. As she passed by in her somewhat inappropriate attire, she thought she heard a few accusing whispers of the word "hypocrite"; but she boldly continued to squeeze her way through the rough Galileans and eventually found herself a spot not far from where the rabbi had just begun to open his lips.

The Gospels record that Christ freed Mary Magdalene

from evil spirits, but they do not tell us how this took place. Based upon the testimony of others who have been liberated from evil spirits by Christ, we can try to imagine Mary's first encounter with him, as she caught a glimpse of his face as he glanced in her direction. In that brief instant of eye contact with the Messiah, eternal life began for Mary Magdalene. Her heart experienced something that it had never known before. As his penetrating gaze rested momentarily upon her, a holy sense of reverence gripped her soul; for an instant she was awestruck. As he began to speak he would regularly look directly into her eyes, and he seemed to be gazing right through them, into the very depths of her soul. Never had a man looked at her in such a way. In his gaze there was nothing that made her feel insecure. Every man she knew either looked at her in a way that made her feel worthless or looked at her as if she were an object he was desperately longing to possess, but in these eyes there was something different. Although she felt unworthy to look into his eyes she was unable to turn away. His gaze reminded her of the way her father used to look upon her as he would carry her in his arms and tell her how precious she was. It was the purest look of a father into the eyes of his little girl, and it made her feel safe. She felt as though the presence of this man was making her into a child once again, restoring to her something that she had lost long ago. Later on she would say that it was like being looked at by God himself, and yet this was truly a man that she saw before her eyes. With every word he spoke, peace poured forth like a fountain of light into her spirit.

Setting the captive free

As her soul now felt more and more drawn to embrace that spiritual light which surrounded the man of God, all of a sudden she was aware of another contrary movement holding her back. A darkness from deep within her was trying to engulf the light drawing her to itself. Unsettling thoughts brought back the sense of fear and panic she had experienced earlier, and an interior confusion began to block out the sound of the teacher's voice. This inner noise gradually became like the cacophony of several ugly voices. These voices were one with her own inner voice, with her own thoughts, and yet she hated them. It was as though some enemy was imprisoning her from deep within her very self.

With these thoughts the memory of her sins came flooding back, and against her own will accused herself of their gravity and the utter impossibility of ever finding God's forgiveness. A river of sad and miserable images of shameful things she had done went racing through her mind and caused a deep movement of despair to run through her entire being. This sickening feeling she had already experienced in the past, especially just before those darkest moments when her life seemed to sink to its lowest depths. A painful weight of guilt too heavy to bear discouraged her to such a degree that she felt paralysed, as though her freedom had vanished. In these moments she felt certain that she had gone too far ever to seek forgiveness from God or to return to her family. To live according to the Law of God was no longer possible for her, and since she was destined to be cut off from the

Holy People of Israel, she would conclude, she might as well continue to live the way she had been living.

In the past this despair would leave her with dark desires for total self-destruction, but this time it was different. Even though these thoughts were perhaps stronger than ever before, the man in front of her seemed even stronger. As she glanced towards him again, a spark of hope returned, and now his previously gentle presence seemed to become power itself. He was as though anointed with the power of the Most High, and she felt called to put her trust in his power to save her from the darkness within. Her entire body was now trembling and covered in a cold sweat, but somehow she summoned the last bit of strength she had and rejected this inner darkness, choosing to put her confidence in the light that came from Jesus. As she did so the trembling stopped, and it seemed as though the hope that came from him was binding and overthrowing the despair within her. She did not understand what was happening in her heart, but she knew that because of the power going out from this man everything would be fine; she could dare to hope once again. Faith, she knew, was something that related to God alone, but she felt that she must somehow put her faith in this man of God too. With the arrival of this intuition peace began to return to her soul.

The Teacher continued to speak to the crowds, but now it seemed as though he was speaking to her alone, speaking not to her mind but right into the very depths of her heart. He spoke now of the mercy of God, of how he had been sent to seek out and save the lost, of how the Lord looks with preferential love upon a humble and contrite heart, of how sinners could dare to approach the Most High and return home justified. His words entered into her heart like no words she had ever heard before. His words seemed as though they were taking life within her and coming to dwell in her forever, and as she welcomed them into her heart the other accusing thoughts began to disappear. The truth of what he was saying could not possibly be doubted or resisted. It would be easier now to doubt her own existence than to doubt the mercy of God, and within her welled up the words "Lord, have mercy on me a sinner." As she repeated these words over and over again, the dark heavy weight that for almost as long as she could remember had seemed to be crushing the very spirit within her suddenly lifted. She felt true freedom for the first time in her life, and it was something very different from the reckless freedom she had proudly flaunted, while all the time she had really been enslaved to sin.

The chains of evil that had bound her heart were broken, the darkness that had trapped her within her very self was gone, and she experienced not just freedom but pure joy too. She felt as though the rabbi's words were cleansing her, as though his mere presence was making her innocent once again, and now an unshakeable hope in God came flooding through her soul. The sun had risen over her life, and it would never be dark again. Soon the crowds would part, but she would remain, fixed to the spot by a heavenly peace. The hours passed like minutes, and her soul went on resting in the love of the Spirit of God. When the ecstatic experience eventually drew to a close, she opened her eyes and found herself all alone and with only one thought: to find the mysterious man of God, to cling to him and never let him go.

As she finally rose to her feet and began to cross the green hills of Galilee, in the direction of the lake that looks like a giant mirror for the sun, a tear streamed from her eye. The heavenly moment had begun to fade away, and the reality of her life came back into focus. She was a sinner: she had done things that the mere thought of now caused her to blush; she had done things that now she could not even understand. Why had she lived so shamefully? It all seemed so unreasonable and pointless to her now. It was as though these things had somehow been done by another person, and to recall them was like looking back into the tomb of that person who was now dead and gone. A new existence had begun the moment she had looked into those mysterious eyes. These sins belonged to her and she was sorry for every last one of them, but in some way she felt as though the guilt of them no longer belonged to her. She began to weep, not because she felt ashamed and knew that she would forever have to bear the burden of her reputation, but rather because she realised that all along God had been there.

From the moment she glimpsed the face of that holy man, she knew that the God he represented was good. She had always felt that the Creator was a harsh judge, to whom she could not dare to draw close, but now she truly understood the words of the Psalm that she had heard so often in her youth but that had always left her baffled: "The Lord is gracious and merciful, slow to anger and abounding in mercy" (Ps 145:8). Now the truth of these words was as clear to her mind as the daylight. She wept because she somehow felt that she had made her good God weep. As she walked towards Magdala, as evening began to fall, her tears continued to flow, but they were accompanied by the inner conviction that no matter what she had done, the good God would forgive her and give her a second chance at life. She was still surrounded by the merciful love of the Lord, which seemed to be carried into the world by his presence.

The one who loved much

This imagined undocumented first encounter between Magdalene and Christ allows us to understand the first time they meet in the Gospels, when Mary displays extraordinary gratitude and love towards Jesus.

> One of the Pharisees asked him to eat with him, and he went into the Pharisee's house, and sat at table. And behold, a woman of the city, who was a sinner, when she learned that he was sitting at table in the Pharisee's house, brought an alabaster flask of ointment, and standing behind him at his feet, weeping, she began to wet his feet with her tears, and wiped them with the hair of her head, and kissed his feet, and anointed them with the ointment. Now when the Pharisee who had invited him saw it, he said to himself, "If this man were a prophet, he would have known who and what sort of woman this is who is touching him, for she is a sinner." (Lk 7:36–39)

Could this woman be Mary Magdalene, come to thank the Lord for liberating her from evil and sin? This interpretation would explain the Lord's reason for telling his host the parable of the two debtors and for his statement: "Therefore I tell you, her sins, which are many, are forgiven, for she loved much; but he who is forgiven little, loves little" (7:47). If this text recounted the first meeting of Jesus and Mary Magdalene it would be difficult to make sense of this statement of Christ and of the unusual attitude of this woman. She appears to have already received some kind of liberation, and the absolution Jesus gives her appears to be an expression of what has already happened in her soul. According to Luke, Mary Magdalene, along with the other women who provide for Christ, serves the Lord out of gratitude for being liberated or healed by him, and in his account of the anointing at the Pharisee's house we see the first signs of that gratitude. André Feuillet concludes that on a purely exegetical level it seems highly probable that the first anointing is not the first encounter between Jesus and the sinful woman.[5] He observes that the woman is expressing a deep love that the passage alone does not explain.

It is important to note the context that Luke provides as the prelude to the anointing. He explains that the Pharisees and the lawyers had chosen not to receive the baptism of John. In this way they had rejected the plan of God for themselves and consequently were incapable of recognising Jesus as Saviour (cf. Lk 7:29–30). Why did they reject the baptism of John? It was a baptism of repentance, and in order to receive it they needed to acknowledge their own sinfulness and to plunge themselves into the

---

[5] André Feuillet, "Les Deux Onctions Faites sur Jésus, et Marie-Madeleine", *Revue Thomiste*, LXXV, 1975, p. 379.

Jordan waters alongside the tax collectors and the other public sinners. Because they could not humble themselves to acknowledge their own need of God's mercy, they now find themselves in opposition to the Saviour. It is probable that although this particular Pharisee has invited Jesus to his home, he is still not immune to this blindness to personal guilt before God.

Luke uses this context to introduce to us Saint Mary Magdalene, who is fully aware of her need of mercy and whose attitude is the polar opposite of the Pharisee's. She is so pleasing to Christ because in her sinfulness she simply allows herself to be saved by the Saviour. Now Jesus uses her attitude to give the world a new spiritual principle:

> And Jesus answering said to him, "Simon, I have something to say to you." And he answered, "What is it, Teacher?" "A certain creditor had two debtors; one owed five hundred denarii, and the other fifty. When they could not pay, he forgave them both. Now which of them will love him more?" Simon answered, "The one, I suppose, to whom he forgave more." And he said to him, "You have judged rightly." Then turning toward the woman he said to Simon, "Do you see this woman? I entered your house, you gave me no water for my feet, but she has wet my feet with her tears and wiped them with her hair. You gave me no kiss, but from the time I came in she has not ceased to kiss my feet. You did not anoint my head with oil, but she has anointed my feet with ointment. Therefore I tell you, her sins, which are many, are forgiven, for she loved much; but he who is forgiven little, loves little." And he said to her, "Your sins are for-

given." Then those who were at table with him began to say among themselves, "Who is this, who even forgives sins?" And he said to the woman, "Your faith has saved you; go in peace." (Lk 7:40–50)

Thus it was that Jesus Christ corrected our understanding of the relationship between God and man. Contrary to what the Pharisees may think, sinners can truly become saints! In fact they may even have an advantage over the apparently upright scribe or Pharisee. It is no longer the self-righteous person who prides himself on following the Law to the letter who can think that he is just before the Lord, but rather the one who knows he is a poor sinner in need of God's mercy. This attitude alone makes us capable of receiving grace. To believe that one has already reached holiness without the help of Christ is not only an illusion but a dangerous spiritual sickness that can prove to be eternally fatal. We have need of only one thing to receive salvation in Christ: to know deep down that we are in need of it!

Sinners have a spiritual vision that Pharisees do not have. They look at Christ, and their humility allows them to perceive in him their only hope of salvation. The Pharisee sees merely the man, whereas the lost sheep sees the Good Shepherd! The poor lost sheep in this passage has pointed out to the world a safe refuge for sinners, namely, at the feet of Jesus Christ. The boldness of her actions has taught us about the confidence we can have in Christ's mercy. Everybody else may despise us, but at his feet we will always find welcome, never rejection. The Lord who had just beforehand been deeply moved by compassion upon seeing a widow's tears now shows that he is also moved by the repentant tears of a sinner. He is the "friend of sinners" (see Luke 15:2) who comes to their defence when they are attacked by the accuser, and the joy of his heart is to bring them to the happiness of hearing the words: "Your sins are forgiven. . . . Go in peace!"

According to the logic of Christ's parable, once sinners experience the liberation from their debt of guilt, gratitude for the divine mercy will enkindle in their hearts a fire of love that far surpasses the lukewarm ritualism of one who has never authentically experienced his need to be forgiven. Mary's display of love is a clear indication that she has interiorly experienced the loving mercy of the Lord. The history of the Church is full of examples of great sinners who, like her, have become great saints. The story of Magdalene is a source of hope for the broken, and it is unfortunate that modern exegesis has deprived so many people of this hope. We sinners desire concrete proof that we can truly become holy and the life-story of this wonderful woman gives us biblical certainty that not only can we be saved but we can actually be numbered among Christ's greatest friends in heaven.

In the nineteenth century a famous French Dominican, Blessed Jean-Joseph Lataste, who had been plagued by severe health problems, was granted the privilege of kissing the skull of Saint Mary Magdalene, and in the moment he did so he received an insight about the Virgin Mary and Mary Magdalene, who were standing side by side at the foot of the Cross: the first was perfect innocence and the second was perfect penitence. He understood that in the New Covenant the greatest sinners have the power to become the greatest saints and to be counted among the most faithful disciples of Christ. At the moment Christ needs friends the most, the lukewarm will be nowhere to be seen. Only innocence or profound penitence can stay faithful to the end.[6]

After receiving this great insight, Fr. Lataste's health problems left him and he began to visit troubled women in prison, with the intention of offering them spiritual retreats and bringing them directly before Jesus in the Blessed Sacrament. So astounded was he by their response to eucharistic adoration and the humble sincerity of their confessions that he decided to found a religious order called Bethany, which they could enter as soon as they were released. Magdalene was welcomed back with open arms by her family in Bethany after her conversion, and Lataste wanted to create a spiritual family that could welcome modern Magdalenes who had been saved by Christ while in prison. The community of the Dominican sisters of Bethany was a great success and spread to several different countries. The first vows were taken on the Feast of Saint Mary Magdalene in 1868. These ex-criminals who were despised by society were loved by Christ, and among them there began to emerge beautiful flowers of holiness. This should not surprise us when we consider that the first saint of the New Covenant, canonised by Jesus himself just before he died on Calvary, was the good thief. His direct entrance into heaven at the moment of death was a testimony to the transforming power of Christ's blood and a sign of things to come!

[6] *L'Année dominicaine* 1859–1860, p. 327.

Purity that makes pure

Simon the Pharisee immediately recognised Mary Magdalene as a well-known sinful woman; according to the Law of Moses, mere physical contact with such a person would make one ritually impure for a certain period of time. Since Jesus was the person she had approached, he was probably expecting the Lord to drive this unclean woman away from him; then the Pharisee could have insisted that she leave his home and never return again. How scandalised he was to see that Jesus let this woman touch him. Simon concluded that Jesus could not be a prophet, because a true prophet would have the spiritual sensitivity to perceive what kind of woman she was.

Here and elsewhere, however, Jesus teaches the world that it is not physical contact with a sinful person that makes one unclean before God but rather the pride and the wickedness that come from the heart. He shows that the judgements we make of sinners are not only unjust but very often incorrect. As we see the broken alabaster jar lying at his feet, we are reminded that Jesus is the anointed king of Israel and of all creation. A king in the Old Testament would have to pronounce judgement on difficult cases of justice arising among the people, and here Jesus shows that he has the authority to pronounce a far deeper judgement. He will judge the eternal fate of the living and the dead, and in this scene he demonstrates that his divine gaze will one day pierce the heart of every man and expose the truth of how each soul appears before God. If the Gospel texts are anything to go by, we can expect to be very surprised when the Day of Judgement reveals the truth about human hearts. "The tax collectors and the harlots go into the kingdom of God" (Mt 21:31) more easily than those who might appear as righteous to the world and themselves.

The Lord allowed the sinful woman to approach him because it is in this contact with the real bodily presence of the Word made flesh that one is sanctified. The Pharisee, not really knowing who Christ was and thinking of the ordinary sinful tendencies of human beings, could look upon this with only great suspicion. Like the Pharisee, certain people who read this text, who are conscious of their own sinful tendencies and who do not really know Christ, have insinuated that there may have been some kind of impropriety between Jesus and the woman. From this have flowed numerous theories about a carnal relationship between the Lord and Saint Mary Magdalene. The promoters of such theories have one thing in common: they do not understand that Jesus Christ is God Incarnate! He is the Holy of Holies, purer than the angels in body and soul and the only marriage he has come into the world to establish is that between God and mankind. The sacred humanity of Christ is the very fountain of grace and purity for all of the great saints, who because of his impeccable holiness were empowered to live lives free from the blemish of grave sin. During Christ's earthly life his adversaries desperately sought to find some sin to hold against him, but all they could come up with were a few distortions of certain statements he had made. So immaculate was his life that nobody at that time would have believed he could be guilty of any base sin. If accusing him of sexual impropriety never entered the minds of the people who hated him the most two thousand years ago, it is foolish to do so today.

Whenever the Lord encounters what is impure, or perceived to be impure, he transmits to it his very own purity. He allowed the woman with a persistent flow of blood to touch his garment, and in the moment she did her ailment was completely healed (Mk 5:28–30). The woman who touched Christ in this way did so without his consent, and she must have been terrified when Jesus stopped and asked who had done it for she knew that she was making him ritually impure. She had not actually broken the Law of Moses, however, because in the moment she touched him her haemorrhage ceased, and Christ praised her holy audacity and faith. Jesus also touched the body of a leper, which would normally have made him unclean for ritual worship; but he contracted no impurity even in this legalistic sense for in the moment he touched him the man was no longer a leper. He went away with his flesh made perfect once again (Mk 1:40–45). Jesus even touched a dead body, perhaps the most ritually impure thing he could possibly have done, but he contracted no impurity for in the moment he touched the corpse the young man was alive once again (Luke 7:14–15).

When the sinful woman in the Gospel of Luke comes into physical contact with Jesus, there is no transmission of her sin to him; rather, she is made whole once again. Her soul, which was dead, rises to a new life of holiness. She falls at his feet a public sinner, and she rises as the prototype of all those who pass from sin to sanctity. As her repentant tears were bathing Christ's feet, power was going out from his heart and the divine gift of compunction was washing her soul whiter than snow. Truly does he pronounce the words: "Your sins are forgiven." There is no need to add "Go and sin no more" for this daughter of Abraham has been renewed by Love. A great master of the spiritual life, Cardinal Pierre de Bérulle, used to say that what the power of Christ's words accomplished in the soul of Magdalene was nothing short of a miracle. Christ did mighty works to make men stop and wonder and then miracles for the angels to behold. The greatest of the first kind was the resurrection of the body of Lazarus, the greatest of the second kind was the resurrection of the soul of Magdalene.

Jesus says nothing in vain, and from the very start of Mary's conversion he describes her as the one "who loved much". Cardinal de Bérulle observes that she begins at the point of perfection, which is the end of the journey of holiness for other souls.[7] Her conversion is total and her response to grace perfect. She passes from death to life in abundance, from vanity to truth, from self-love to purest love for Christ. The resurrection and transformation of her soul becomes the joy of Christ's heart. The ancient litany of Saint Mary Magdalene, still used for the annual procession of her relics, praises the total transformation of her heart with beautiful imagery:

[7] Pierre de Bérulle, *Élévation sur Sainte Madeleine* (Paris: Éditions du Cerf, 1987), pp. 44‑55.

Saint Mary Magdalene, pray for us . . .
You, who carried the alabaster jar of perfume,
   pray for us.
You, who from dark clay became purest crystal,
   pray for us.
Diamond, passing from the dust to the light,
   pray for us.
Transformed into a vessel of glory, pray for us.
Sparkling pearl, pray for us.
Blazing Torch for the whole world, pray for us . . .
Apostle to the Apostles, pray for us . . .
Sweet Advocate of penitents, pray for us . . .

When seven demons are expelled from a soul they normally try to return at some point, each one bringing with it seven more, even worse than itself, but they dare not try to come back to the pure soul of Magdalene. Now her heart contains too much love, for evil to dwell in it again. The love for Christ in her soul is itself an unceasing exorcism, and even today her very bones have been known to free souls bound by attachment to sin. In the Middle Ages she was held up as the biblical model of perfect contrition, a rare grace in which the soul is cleansed and restored in an instant and there remains no reparation to be made for past sins. The purity of this kind of contrition given by the Holy Spirit is perfect because it is based on love for God alone, and this love for God in her heart was no mere passing reality. A fire was enkindled within her when she first met Jesus Christ, and nothing would ever be able to quench that holy fire once it began to burn.

Blessed Cardinal John Henry Newman, who was a firm

believer in the identification theory, praises Magdalene, the queen of penitents, as one who displays the most passionate kind of love for Christ. He notices that the love of lifelong faithful souls is often more calm and subdued, but the love of converts is a devouring flame that consumes their hearts and spills over into the most zealous acts of devotion. Where divine mercy abounds in the life of a soul, grateful love will also abound in due measure. Penitents will often go to war on the spirit of the world, which once held them captive, and will cling to their Saviour with a most ardent and impetuous kind of love. The saintly Cardinal Newman lauds the magnanimous soul of Mary Magdalene and what happened in it after she arose from washing the feet of Jesus with her tears:

> Henceforth, my brethren, love was to her, as to St. Augustine and to St. Ignatius of Loyola afterwards (great penitents in their own time), as a wound in the soul, so full of desire as to become anguish. She could not live out of the presence of Him in whom her joy lay: her spirit languished after Him, when she saw Him not; and waited on Him silently, reverently, wistfully, when she was in His blissful Presence. We read of her, on one occasion, sitting at His feet, and listening to His words; and He testified to her that she had chosen that best part which should not be taken away from her. And, after His resurrection, she, by her perseverance, merited to see Him even before the Apostles.[8]

---

[8] John Henry Newman, "Purity and Love", quoted in *The Treasury of Catholic Wisdom*, John Hardon, S.J., ed. (San Francisco: Ignatius Press, 1995), p. 551.

"Your faith has saved you!"

Jesus looks with love at this poor despised sinner and tells her that it is her faith in him that has saved her. We might also translate these consoling words of Christ as "Your faith has healed you" or "Your faith has made you whole" or even "Your faith has made you safe." However one chooses to translate it, the emphasis is upon the interior disposition of the sinful woman. Jesus has saved her himself, but he proclaims before all that it is really her faith in him that has saved her. Earlier on, she had the intuition to put her faith and trust in this man of God, and now Jesus, whose gaze sees into the depths of the spirit, confirms that her interior response to that intuition has saved her and made her whole once again. She has been "made safe" and removed from all spiritual danger by her faith and trust in Christ.

It is important for us all to be aware that we receive grace from Jesus in proportion to our interior receptivity. In chapter 8 of the Gospel of Luke, we see the woman with the haemorrhage touch Jesus and receive a miraculous healing. Immediately Christ turned and asked who had touched him. Peter was perplexed by the question and rightly pointed out to him that whole crowds of people were touching him. But it is as though Jesus is saying that while many people touch him, somebody has really "touched" him (Lk 8:45–47). In other words, somebody has touched him not only with the fingertips but also with deep faith, and this touch released healing grace from his heart. As one of the Fathers of the Church points out, the woman first touched Christ with her mind and then with her hands.[9] Similarly Magdalene receives the grace of healing and salvation because of her interior disposition of faith in Christ.

At the celebration of Holy Mass, many people can "touch" Christ in Holy Communion, but only those with profound faith in his Real Presence will receive the graces that are available. The interior disposition of the heart must correspond to the words of worship on our lips. All who attend the eucharistic sacrifice truly come in contact with Jesus, like the crowds in Capernaum, but not all go away sanctified by the encounter. In the same way, when we approach Jesus seeking forgiveness in the Sacrament of Penance, we will receive deeper graces of transformation if the disposition of our hearts is pleasing in his sight. There is only one Saviour, but he does not save us without the interior cooperation of our minds and hearts.

The prophetess of love

The expression of love on the part of Mary Magdalene in this text may seem to her sophisticated spectators like the somewhat embarrassing gesture of a vulgar woman who has little self-restraint and who is inclined to go to extremes in all she does. The words of Jesus reveal, however, that something far deeper is taking place, and it is rather the beginning of the prophetic vocation of a saint.

A prophet is one through whom God speaks to the world. At times a prophet speaks words that come from

[9] Thomas Aquinas, *Catena Aurea*, Luke 8.

God and at other times he communicates through inspired gestures. Jeremiah and Ezekiel are well known for their nonverbal prophetic messages (Jer 27–28; Ezek 4:1–3). Normally this kind of prophecy either announces the arrival of some extremely important event for the people or has the character of a rebuke for those to whom it is addressed. A prophet will often have to warn people of how they have offended the Lord and what they must do to correct their offence.

Later on, Mary's actions will announce the arrival of a most solemn event for the world, the death and the burial of Christ, but in this particular text her gestures have been inspired by the Holy Spirit so that she might correct the Pharisee and repair the insult by which he has offended Christ: his failure to give a proper welcome to the most honourable guest he could ever host in his home. Perhaps the Pharisee did not want to appear as though he was a disciple of Jesus, whose ways were unorthodox to say the least, and perhaps the invitation he extended to Christ was partly motivated by a desire to scrutinise him in the company of his friends. We cannot know his motives, but it is clear that for some reason he chose not to show the Lord the signs of respect due to a guest of honour. Not only did Magdalene repair the insult and accomplish what was left undone by the Pharisee, but she did so in a far more beautiful way than the Pharisee could ever have done.

Jesus compares and contrasts what the Pharisee should have done with what this woman actually did: he should have washed Christ with mere water from the well, but her love has called forth a stream of tears to cleanse his feet; he should have embraced Jesus at the door, but she kisses his feet unceasingly (and the Greek word used here for "kiss" is the word that expresses the deepest feelings of love); he should have anointed the head of Jesus with oil, but she has gone further and anointed his very feet, not only with oil but with what can be translated as "perfumed oil". Everything she does is better than anything the Pharisee could ever have done, and thus perfect reparation has been made to the divine dignity.

A nonverbal prophecy always requires an interpretation, and here the Eternal Word himself provides one. He looks at the woman, to draw attention to her gestures, and speaks to the Pharisee as he holds her up as an example of love for all present (Lk 7:44). Though they may look down upon her as one humiliated in the eyes of men, she is now exalted in the eyes of the Lord. We will see that this will not be the last time Mary's prophetic love will be called upon to repair the sins of others and to proclaim deep mysterious truths. Love speaks its own language, and here the biblical "prophetess of love" has audaciously proclaimed the kind of respect and gratitude one should have in the presence of the Messiah. Furthermore, her gestures of love here are so extraordinary that it seems she has some kind of intuition of the divinity of Christ. She has hardly understood the doctrine of his divinity intellectually, but her heart has perceived that this man is worthy of an honour that no other man, not even the holiest of men, could ever merit; therefore she instinctively offers him a kind of adoration. When he looked into her eyes, she knew that this was not the look of a mere mortal, and her heart could not restrain itself from offering him the type of adoration due to God alone!

If only all hearts were as docile to the Holy Spirit as this humble, contrite heart. Long before almost everybody else in the Gospels, the prophetess of love becomes a fervent adorer, and by her gestures at least she proclaims that Jesus is divine. Another nonverbal teaching her example gives us is that the Lord is infinitely merciful, and by her confidence in approaching his holy presence she gives hope to those tempted to despair because of their sins. Prostrate at his feet Magdalene proclaims to us all: "Be not afraid. In the heart of Christ there is nothing but Love!"

From penitent to benefactor

Mary Magdalene is one of those saints who can appeal to all categories of Christians, for she provides an example to us all, regardless of our vocations. At times she is the repentant sinner, at times the perfect contemplative, the one who loves much. At times she is an apostle, running to proclaim the Good News, at times she is simply heartbroken and grieving. Whatever our state in life or whatever we are going through, this saint has something to say to us. Her personality is universal and contains the rare but admirable mixture of reserve and audacity—a capacity for deep intimacy with the Lord and intense activity in his service. Certain souls transcend all of our psychological categories and our narrow ways of understanding, especially when such souls have been transformed by divine grace. We have all met the greatest extroverts living in cloistered convents as model contemplatives, and seemingly shy characters who explode into powerful preachers when the Church gives them a mandate. Grace builds upon but also elevates and transforms human nature.

As well as being the prototype of contemplatives, converts and penitents, Magdalene is the prototype of lay people whose generosity has allowed the Church to do great things down through the centuries. For example, when the French government pillaged all of the Church's property during the Reign of Terror, it was thanks to the extraordinary generosity of a lay woman that Father Henri Lacordaire was able to repurchase the Dominican property of Saint Maximin and to bring the Dominican Order back to accomplish the mission the pope had given them there at the basilica and the grotto of la Sainte Baume. Without such generosity who knows what would have become of these sacred shrines, not to mention all the people who have been converted or sanctified through them.

Shortly after her conversion Mary Magdalene realised that Jesus Christ had not so much as a single silver coin in his possession. In order to find a coin to pay the temple tax he once had to have recourse to the mouth of a fish (Mt 17:24–27). He lived like the birds in the sky, counting on his heavenly Father to inspire generous souls to provide for his needs. Mary felt called to be one of those souls, and after having introduced her old friend Joanna to Christ, so that she too could at last find true joy, together they would make sure that the Lord, who was the very Light of the World, would never have to want for anything:

Soon afterward he went on through cities and villages, preaching and bringing the good news of the kingdom of God. And the Twelve were with him, and also some women who had been healed of evil spirits and infirmities: Mary, called Magdalene, from whom seven demons had gone out, and Joanna, the wife of Chuza, Herod's steward, and Susanna, and many others, who provided for them out of their means. (Lk 8:1-3)

3

Perfect Image of the New Eve

One of the most memorable events in the life of Mary Magdalene was the moment she first glimpsed the face of Jesus Christ, but there was another unforgettable moment etched into her memory—the moment Jesus first presented her to his own Mother, also called Mary. With Magdalene's spiritual sensitivity, how beautiful the Mother of Jesus appeared to her. She was gentleness incarnate. The woman was utterly magnificent, beautiful in every way, and her eyes were filled with light, like the innocent eyes of a child. She did nothing to attract attention to herself. She seemed like a precious jewel made to be gazed upon by God alone.

The women Magdalene had known in the court of Herod were also beautiful, among the most physically beautiful to be found, and yet in their desire to appear beautiful, so as to be admired by others, they actually lost something of their true beauty. They wanted to be like goddesses, put upon a pedestal to be adored. As soon as another more beautiful woman appeared, they would resent and despise her in their hearts. Magdalene could see now that vanity actually spoiled true beauty and caused nothing but spitefulness and jealousy. With the Mother of Jesus, on the other hand, by not seeking to be admired she became even more beautiful.

What a rare and delightful creature Mary was. Her beauty came from deep within her soul; it was the beauty of love. Magdalene would look upon her and weep that she had thrown her innocence away. Yet the presence of the Mother never discouraged her but brought with it a deep sense of hope. In her company, Magdalene never felt judged, but rather loved, respected and understood. She wanted nothing now but to become like this woman clothed in the light of holiness and who had at last shown her what feminine beauty truly is. She would treasure every minute she was privileged to spend in the presence of this Mystical Rose, whose warm and welcoming heart seemed to contain nothing but love. In her was nothing ugly or insincere, and Magdalene could only marvel at this woman filled with grace!

The Lord Jesus gave Mary Magdalene the singular privilege of spending much time in the company of his Mother, and this is why we find them together at the foot of the Cross (Jn 19:25). Jesus wanted Magdalene to learn many things from his Mother's example and words. It was as though he wanted to see a reflection of his own dear Mother in her soul. Spending time in the presence of this woman had a deep effect upon Magdalene, and little by little she indeed came to resemble her. Her life had once been a shipwreck because of the ancient sin of Eve, but now she was chosen to be the first woman in history to be recreated in the image of the New Eve.

The characteristic attitude that we admire in the life of the Blessed Virgin Mary is her attentiveness to Jesus

Christ. She is constantly pondering in her heart whatever Jesus says and does (Lk 2:51). In Scripture we see her already meditating deeply upon what would later become for us the joyful mysteries of the Rosary. God is revealing himself to the world in the Person of Jesus Christ, but few are the souls who are receptive to this revelation, who give the Word of God the attention he deserves. Our Lady did this perfectly in the name of all of mankind. It is little wonder that the next time we come across Mary Magdalene in the Gospels, we can see that she has learned a secret from the Mother of Jesus. She has learned what it is that pleases Jesus the most, namely, souls who are attentive to him and to every word that comes forth from his mouth. Saint Thomas Aquinas once wrote that what Jesus loved most in John the Beloved Disciple was the perspicacity of his mind, the fact that he would listen to what Jesus taught and then continue to meditate upon it so as to penetrate its depths.[1] This meditative attitude characteristic of beloved disciples was first lived to perfection by the Blessed Virgin Mary in the holy house of Nazareth. It is this same Marian attitude that we will soon find in the heart of Saint Mary Magdalene.

In the next Gospel text where we can behold the saint, we find ourselves within the last six months of the earthly life of Christ, somewhere between the Feast of Tabernacles and the Feast of Dedication, probably towards the end of the month of November.[2] It has been about a year and a half since Mary Magdalene first laid

---

[1] Thomas Aquinas, *Commentary on John*, no. 2639.
[2] Andres Fernandez, S.J., *The Life of Christ* (Westminster, Md.: Newman Press, 1958), p. 71.

eyes upon the one who would raise her soul from the
dead. During the course of these past eighteen months
she has been swept along by a chain of events hitherto
unparalleled in human history. As she looked back on
this adventure that had become her daily life, she could
only give thanks for having seen things she could never
have even imagined before. In her youth she craved excitement and an escape from the dull life of Bethany, but
now she knew that there was nothing in this world as exciting as the company of Jesus Christ. It is not the excitement of the hippodrome that he brought, but something
far deeper and more powerful than that. Those who have
learned to contemplate and to adore Jesus Christ thirst
no more for the vanities of the world (Jn 6:35).

The intense period of Christ's missionary activity that
she had entered started out very well. For the first nine or
ten months that she knew him, Jesus had all of the Galilean
crowds mesmerised by his words and works. She had lost
count of the number of miraculous healings she had seen
with her own eyes. The sons of Zebedee had also told her
about some other stunning miracles they had witnessed,
including the little girl he had brought back from the
dead (Mk 5:21–43). On more than one occasion Jesus
had calmed storms at sea, not to mention all the times
he had calmed the spiritual storms stirred up in the souls
of the possessed (Mk 4:35–5:20; Mt 14:32). Apart from
certain narrow-minded Pharisees and scribes who criticised his apparently original interpretations of points of
the Law, in the early days everybody was in amazement at
the Prophet from Nazareth. The crowds followed him in
hundreds and at times thousands (Mk 6:31–44). Some-

times he had to hide himself in the countryside so as to have a moment in peace to pray (Mk 1:45).

All of this excitement had reached its highest point when he took a few loaves and a few fish and used them to feed thousands of people who had come to hear him preach. After that spectacular event, the multitudes went from speaking of him as a great prophet to proclaiming him their king (Jn 6:14–15). Could this really be the long-awaited "shoot from the stump of Jesse" that would govern the nations (Is 11:1)? God himself seemed to be confirming his anointing by the most marvellous signs. It was becoming clear to many that he was the first man in history ever to accomplish all the messianic signs and wonders. Yet no sooner had this happened than the popularity of Jesus underwent a setback, as a result of an unusual sermon in which he said something about eating his flesh and drinking his blood (Jn 6:22–71). Even some of his most sincere disciples were scandalized, and after that fateful day in the synagogue of Capernaum the fervour of the people of Galilee began to wane.

He had spoken well until then, but on that day he had said things that many perceived to be not only shocking but also blasphemous (Jn 6:60). He spoke of himself as having come down from heaven so as to become bread to be eaten. When given an opportunity to recant or clarify his words, he insisted that this was a truth that must be accepted if one wanted to live forever (Jn 6:53–54). The Pharisees used the confusion created by this sermon to promote their theory about Jesus of Nazareth. With the help of some scholars from Jerusalem, they had already begun to advance the position that Jesus was not the Christ but rather possessed by an evil spirit (Lk 11:15; Mk 3:22). In an accusation that deeply grieved the heart of Magdalene, they now spread the rumour throughout Galilee, saying he worked wonders so as to deceive people into thinking he was the Messiah. They insinuated that he was trying to change the Law of Moses, to allow for the idolatrous adoration of himself and eventually to practises abhorrent to the Jewish mind, such as drinking his lifeblood (Gen 9:4). They pointed out to the people that only God would have the right to say such things about himself and the authority to reinterpret Mosaic Law. He had even gone so far as to say something that no man had ever had the audacity to say before: that he could forgive sins (Mk 2:10). With statements of this kind there were only two logical conclusions that could be drawn: either he was somehow divine or he was an impostor. The poor in spirit invariably chose to believe the former, while the Pharisees chose the latter and dragged along with them those who wavered.

In the eight or nine months that had passed since that mysterious and decisive "living bread" sermon in Capernaum, Jesus had lost much support in Galilee. No matter what signs he worked, many people in Capernaum, Chorazin and Bethsaida looked upon him with great suspicion, as though he were a potential danger to them and their loved ones. The more that time went on, the more the Pharisees poisoned their minds with threats of being cursed if they put their faith in Jesus. Following Jesus, they warned, meant breaking away from the safety of the Covenant and being ostracized from the synagogue (Jn 9:22). To be put out of the synagogue would be a living hell for a Jew; and with threats of this kind and other subtle tactics, the religious authorities managed to frighten many people away from Christ.

As though to be free from this oppressive atmosphere for a while, Jesus left Galilee with his friends and went into pagan districts, going as far away as Tyre and Sidon (Mk 7:24). Ironically, many pagans welcomed him with more respect than his own people, and he reproduced for them the miracle of multiplying the loaves and the fish (Mk 8:1–10). Jesus did not remain away from his beloved homeland for too long, however. Along with his disciples, he returned for another tour of intense missionary activity.

A visit to Jerusalem for the Feast of Tabernacles was fraught with danger and tensions provoked by rumours circulated by scribes and Pharisees (Jn 7:30–44). In Judaea people were on the watch for anything Jesus might say that sounded like heresy or blasphemy. They were quick to let him know that for statements the Galilean peasants might tolerate out of ignorance, they would be ready to punish him with death (Jn 8:52–59). Returning to Galilee Jesus continued to bless and work wonders for those humble souls who received him, but he did have some stern words of warning for the towns in which he had done most of his miracles, but which were now treating his message with much scorn and suspicion (Lk 10:13–16). To whom much is given, of him will much be required (Lk 12:48).

Magdalene never ceased to marvel at how gentle he was towards individuals but how firm he was in speaking of sin and its consequences. He seemed to love poor sinners in a special way but had no tolerance for sin whatsoever. His words had the power to bring unshakeable confidence in God's mercy and at the same time such a sense of reverence that you would rather die than ever offend him again. His personality was irresistibly attractive, but at times his holiness made you feel so unworthy of being anywhere near him (Lk 5:8). The faithful disciples clung to him with all of the love in their hearts. His presence had become their one true joy, yet after certain wonders he accomplished they would feel not only amazement but also a kind of holy fear (Mk 10:32). The effect of his presence upon the heart was simply indescribable; it was as though he were some kind of ineffable mystery that transcended ordinary categories of understanding. Trying to explain what he was really like and how he made someone feel seemed to be beyond the power of human words.

Perhaps it was on account of the rejection that his message was now receiving from many in Galilee, especially from those in authority, that the Lord made the decision to move on from there and to go across the Jordan to spend some time working in Perea, an area that some called "Judaea beyond the Jordan" (Mt 19:1). The apostles and some other disciples would accompany him, but he instructed Magdalene to go home to Bethany for a while, so that her family relationships might be fully healed after the years of tension. She had seen her brother and sister several times since her conversion, but she had not yet spent any kind of prolonged period living in Bethany. She was reluctant to spend any considerable length of time away from Jesus, especially now that he would be dwelling so close to hostile Judaea, where real dangers to his life might present themselves. She had already been told that there was talk among those at the highest levels of power in Jerusalem of forming a plot to have him executed for blasphemy (Mt 26:4).

As sorry as she was to leave him at such a time, she knew by now never to question the commands of Christ. The wisdom of what he counselled was always proven in the end. So as they all made their way towards the River Jordan, to cross over into Perea, she parted company from Jesus and the group of disciples and returned to the place where she had spent her childhood. She was welcomed with open arms by Martha and Lazarus, who were eager to hear everything she had seen in the presence of the Lord. In recounting the events of the previous year and a half, Magdalene would weep many tears of love, and after a few weeks at home she realised how much her heart was now pining for Christ's holy presence.

Far away from the Lord, the weeks felt more like months, but soon arrived the happy day when Jesus came for a visit. On their way to Jerusalem for the Feast of Tabernacles, Jesus and his disciples stopped at Bethany to visit their friend Mary and her family. As happy as Magdalene had been to be fully reconciled with her family and to spend some time with them in peace, she was by now consumed with a burning desire to see Jesus once again. Other relationships can bring us happiness in their own way, but once the supernatural joy of an encounter with Jesus Christ has truly been experienced, any separation from him is a source of interior pain. To the soul of an adorer, the Real Presence of Christ is like a fountain of living water in a dry and arid land. By now the unceasing prayers of Mary were for a return to the sweet privilege of being in the company of the Lord. Her prayers were heard. The surprise vision of Jesus appearing at the front door of her sister's house was truly a sight for sore eyes! Here is what happened during the course of his stay in the home of Martha:

> Now as they went on their way, he entered a village; and a woman named Martha received him into her house. And she had a sister called Mary, who sat at the Lord's feet and listened to his teaching. But Martha was distracted with much serving; and she went to him and said, "Lord, do you not care that my sister has left me to serve alone? Tell her then to help me." But the Lord answered her, "Martha, Martha, you are anxious and troubled about many things; one thing is needful. Mary has chosen the good portion, which shall not be taken away from her." (Lk 10:38–42)

"Martha, Martha . . ."

In this text Martha clearly seems to be the woman of the house who welcomes Christ with great hospitality and wants to do everything to make him comfortable. Mary is once again found in the place where we saw her back in the early days of her conversion, namely, at the feet of Christ. This has become her favourite place on earth, and we will find her here again and again in Scripture; and one day we will probably find that she is still at Christ's feet in heaven too! This is the place that expresses her humility and adoration of the Real Presence of Jesus. Luke tells us that she was listening attentively to the Word of Christ, and her posture expresses a disposition of docile obedience. Jewish spirituality is centred upon listening obediently to the commands of the Lord, and here Mary personifies that admirable attitude.

The fact that Luke does not explicitly draw a link between the sinful woman converted in Galilee and the sister of Martha is a stumbling block for many in accepting the identification theory. As mysterious as this may be, we can see that often Scripture uses different names for the same person, without giving any further explanation as to the identity of the person. The tradition has always said that Nathanael is another name for the apostle Bartholomew, but this is not clear in Scripture. Mary of Clopas is at times called Mary of Alphaeus and at times Mary the mother of James. Peter is often called Simon, even after he had received his vocational name from Christ. We are given no reason to explain why Matthew is called Levi by Mark and Luke. Very often different texts that speak of the same person fail to make his identity clear.

There may also be other reasons, however, why Mary is not identified as the once sinful woman. When he decided to write a Gospel, Saint Luke went looking for eyewitness accounts of the events of Christ's life. It is possible that he did not know everything about Mary's life but just wrote down stories as people in different locations recounted them to him. A person living in Galilee might have looked upon Mary as a mere sinful woman, while some people who knew her in Judaea may always have referred to her as the sister of Martha. He may have received the stories about Mary Magdalene from several different sources and the eyewitnesses may simply have recounted the events, with their memories fixed on Christ and his revelation, rather than the names of other characters. The Gospel texts were at first oral traditions, stories passed on from one person to the next, and here is a famous story that Luke received from somebody who might never have known any more about the people involved, but who considered the story worth memorising and sharing.

There was also a custom in the ancient world to protect the reputation of sinners while they were still alive. None of the synoptic Gospels tell us that it was Saint Peter who committed the crime of cutting off the ear of the high priest's servant in the Garden of Gethsemane. Not only would this have made Peter more unpopular in Jerusalem, but it was not a very becoming act for the first pope to have committed. Only John who was writing after the death of Peter tells us who actually did this. Ironically, it was John who also tells us that it was Mary of Bethany who had anointed Christ's feet. Mary was surely still alive when the Gospel of Luke was written, and the evangelist may not have wanted the first public witness of the Resurrection to be exposed as a woman who once had a very bad reputation. In the ancient world many were already criticising Christianity for valuing the testimony of women so highly, and to value the testimony of a woman of this kind would have further damaged the credibility of the message. Luke may have been particularly sensitive to this problem and therefore even in the Resurrection accounts he downplays the role of the women and spends his time describing the later apparitions to men.

Raymond Bruckberger observes that the synoptic evangelists write about the family of Bethany in a very unusual way. They are spoken of with a kind of mysterious discretion because they were so close to Christ, so well respected by many, but so hated in Jerusalem, especially after the resurrection of Lazarus. The synoptic evangelists write of them in a veiled manner, the way we would write of people who live under a totalitarian regime and who may be subject to immediate reprisals if we reveal something carelessly.[3] Luke is writing during the lifetime of this persecuted family, but John, who writes much later, is not subject to the same degree of caution and thus he reveals a little more. He alone tells us exactly what happened in relation to the family of Bethany, and especially Mary, in the last couple of months of Christ's life, while the synoptic evangelists tell us that some anonymous woman in Bethany anointed the Lord. In any case, the Gospel of John seems to counterbalance the ambiguity in Luke's representation of this woman, whose gestures are so unusual and who is always defended by Christ. In this scene she is teaching us some more very important lessons.

An undivided heart

Certain people are driven by deep desire, by an overpowering quest for love. If virtue has not yet brought the body into subjection to the soul, then such people can end up in a most frustrated and disordered state. They seek absolute love with all of their strength but never find it on earth, until they find it in God. When such souls are

---

[3] Raymond Léopold Bruckberger, O.P., *Marie Madeleine* (Paris: La Jeune Parque, 1953), p. 178.

drawn up from the things of the world into the spiritual marriage with God they can become the most extraordinary contemplatives. The passionate desire with which they once clung to creatures in a disordered way is now elevated and channeled into the most intense kind of mystical love for God alone. Such was the spiritual journey of Blessed Charles de Foucauld and Saint Augustine.

The prototype of these conversions is Saint Mary Magdalene. She was a soul created to love intensely; she was guided by her heart and driven by passionate desire. In the moment of her discovery of the love of God in the Person of Christ, the consuming desire of her heart was supernaturalised by grace and finally found the object for which it was created. She clung to God now with all the power of her loving soul, and at times this clinging would be instinctively expressed by her physical attachment to the feet of Christ. She was the model of those who discover the Real Presence of Jesus in the world and who cling to him as the only joy of their hearts. Magdalene became not only the perfect celibate, loving God with a totally undivided heart, but also the perfect contemplative adorer, motivated by nothing but pure supernatural desire.

Christ has his angels to love him in his divinity unveiled in heaven, and on earth he has his angels to love him in the humble exterior that veils the same divinity. In heaven the seraphim, the "burning ones" in Hebrew, have no other mission but to love and adore the thrice-holy God. In the scene portrayed by Luke, Magdalene is like an earthly seraph, consumed with desire for mystical union with God alone. Only in the Real Presence of Christ was her soul at rest, and in her sister's house, despite all that needed to be done, she could do nothing but rest in the light of his presence. The words of Psalm 73:25 have become her own: "Whom have I in heaven but you? And there is nothing upon earth that I desire besides you."

"Do you not care?"

How amusing is the directness of Saint Martha in her way of relating to Christ. Her words here show us the familiarity she had with the Lord and thus the humility with which he must have wielded his divine authority and holiness. Some people are so busy that they seem to speak almost before they think. "Do you not care?" is not the ordinary way one addresses the Messiah, the person she will later call "the Christ, the Son of God" (Jn 11:27); but Martha knows deep down that Jesus is meek and humble of heart. "Are you not concerned?" would be another valid translation of this somewhat impertinent question, which is one that often rises up in the human heart. Life is difficult and it brings all kinds of trials, the reasons for which we will know only in heaven and which are not always the consequences of our sins. Good and innocent people often have many mysterious sufferings to bear.

The devil tempts us into thinking that God abandons us and does not care about our problems. Only through the wisdom that comes from contemplation of the Cross do we learn how untrue this is. Sometimes, however, we question the Lord's concern for us even when our problems stem from our own way of thinking and acting. At times we may be tempted to think that the Lord does not care about how overburdened and stressed we are by the cares of daily life, when in reality there may be something in our own attitude or choice of activity that is removing the peace from our hearts. Sometimes we meet people who have gotten themselves into complicated situations and who have had no real personal relationship with Christ for many years. When they find themselves in a crisis they will often ask why God has let this happen to them, but the truth is, the crisis is the product of their own free will, exercised without any thought for doing the divine will. God in his infinite love is always concerned about our sufferings, but he lets us act freely; and without him we will always get ourselves into difficult situations. Only in doing the will of God do we find true inner peace. Martha's interior disturbance may be at least partially self-inflicted.

Not only does Martha ask Jesus this bold and confrontational question but she also tells him what he should do, namely, to tell Mary to help. Martha was such a good organiser that she would not hesitate to tell even God what he should be thinking and doing. Jesus is not annoyed but calmly responds: "Martha, Martha . . ." In the repetition of her name he shows something of the affection he holds in his heart for this loveable woman; even if he must still rebuke her for attacking the contemplative gift he is giving to her sister.

Martha was expecting Jesus to make her sister learn something about the virtue of service. She had never been able to understand Mary, who always seemed irresponsible and self-absorbed. She would waste her time reading about pagan women of questionable character, and all of this idle nonsense is what so corrupted her mind that her life was in ruins. Martha had always prided herself on being a good daughter of Israel: she was responsible and virtuous, always busy putting things in order and helping anyone in need. For her it was extremely important to provide the very best hospitality whenever a guest arrived. She was indeed very happy that her sister had at last come back onto the right path, but she felt it would still take many years for her to become of some use to the family.

Overly active people do not reason in a spiritual way, and they are often tempted to judge the value of a person's actions based on their apparent utility or productivity. Perhaps Martha was thinking to herself that a word in the ear of Jesus might accelerate the process of Mary's rehabilitation. Since the Master was the only one she seemed to listen to, he might finally be able to teach Mary to be more thoughtful and conscientious, just like Martha herself. Of course Mary would never be much of an organiser, but she might at least be freed from this tendency to waste her time in daydreams. How surprised Martha must have been at the response of Jesus! It was the moment that her self-righteousness was shattered and she began to acquire the virtue of humility. Mary had overtaken her on the path to holiness; she had chosen the better part of loving attentiveness to Christ, and nobody had the right to take that gift from her.

"One thing is needful"

Our Lord understood Mary's soul and knew that although
she might appear to be lazy or indifferent to the needs
of Martha, in reality this was not the case. She was so
utterly absorbed by the mystical light of Christ and the
profundity of his divine teaching, that she almost forgot
everything else. Mary was not thinking of anything but
the privilege of being in the presence of the Master once
again. Mary was not deliberately neglecting her sister, she
was too busy saying to herself what the soldiers in the
Gospel of John would later say out loud: "No man ever
spoke like this man!" (Jn 7:46).

As with the disciples on the road to Emmaus, the heart
of Mary would burn within her whenever Jesus spoke,
and she could not bring herself to leave his company without a struggle. Jesus was an utter marvel, and while he
was present she wanted to do nothing but gaze at him
and receive every single syllable of wisdom he would utter. Every word he spoke was worthy of being mem-
orised and treasured in the heart. Mary is the model
of those whose privileged calling is to live for contemplation of this Word alone; and although the needs of
Martha may seem more pressing, the one with spiritual vision knows that the contemplative vocation is supremely
important.

Saint Gregory the Great spoke of this text as showing
the importance of contemplation, which begins in this
life and goes on for all eternity.

> The two women signify two dimensions of the spiritual
> life. Martha signifies the active life as she busily labours

to honour Christ through her work. Mary exemplifies the contemplative life as she sits attentively to listen and learn from Christ. While both activities are essential to Christian living, the latter is greater than the former. For in heaven the active life terminates, while the contemplative life reaches its perfection.[4]

Activity for the evangelisation and salvation of the world will one day come to an end, but contemplation will never be "taken away" from us. It is a heavenly activity.

Some people receive the grace to understand that the Real Presence of the Word made flesh merits constant attention; and that as urgent as activity may appear, adoration is even more urgent. Mary is an image of those future members of the Church who would understand the importance of perpetual eucharistic adoration. It may look as though she should be serving with Martha, while Christ remains alone for a while, but she is in no doubt that when he is really present somebody should be at his feet.

Jesus implies that Mary has discovered and freely chosen the one thing that is really necessary or needful. This seems to be a reference to the one thing that is indispensable or essential for anyone, namely, to contemplate and love the Lord, but the word is mysterious and may contain a deeper meaning about what is needed when Christ is present.

In Greek this word "needful" or "needed" is related to the word for "lacking" and refers to something important that is absent. It occurs around fifty times in the

---

[4] Gregory the Great, *Moralia* 2, 6.

New Testament, and almost every time it refers to something a person needs but does not have. The Real Presence of the Divine Lord in our churches ought never to
be lacking in adorers, for the living presence of God in
the world needs to be respected. His presence, which is
perpetually adored in heaven, demands to be perpetually
adored on earth too, but in his goodness he will not force
us to do this. He waits for us to choose this good portion
out of love. Very often today the Real Presence of Christ
in our churches meets the real absence of the faithful,
but thankfully there are always a few souls who have the.
supernatural instinct of Mary Magdalene, to know that
somebody "needs" to be attentive to Christ wherever we
still have the joy of his bodily presence among us.

How to receive the Lord "under our roof"

Although this text has always been used to explain the
merit of the contemplative vocation as willed by the Lord,
it is also a simple lesson for us all, whatever our vocation
may be, on the importance of attentiveness to the presence of Christ. The way that Luke describes the scene
makes it clear that Mary has done the will of God in
listening to Christ. He also mentions that "Martha was
distracted." Martha was undoubtedly full of goodwill in
wanting to serve the Lord, but in this particular moment
it seems that Christ wanted to teach and so it was not the
time to do anything but listen. Martha misses this com-
munication from the Lord because she is too distracted,
and often this is true for us. We fail to perceive Christ's
presence and to receive his inspirations because we are

distracted by many things. Advancement in the spiritual life is ultimately learning to be attentive to Christ wherever he is present and active in our lives. This is what permits us to enter into deep union with the divine will. At times Jesus is trying to communicate to us through different events or through the words of another person. At times he is calling out to us for help in the poor and the suffering. We need to have spiritual vision in order to be able to perceive the light of his presence. Saint Teresa of Calcutta would often make the connection between seeing and adoring Jesus in the Eucharist and seeing and loving him in those who are suffering. Gazing upon the sacred Host sharpens our spiritual vision so that we can see Christ wherever he is seeking to be found. In order to be able to see him with the eyes of faith in the Blessed Sacrament we need to cultivate within us the attitude of Mary, not Martha; we need to rid our minds of distractions and concentrate upon him with the interior gaze of the heart.

The highest and most sublime moment of encountering Christ's presence in our lives is when we receive him into our very bodies in Holy Communion. In this passage Martha literally receives Jesus "under her roof", and this image calls to mind the words that prepare us to receive the Lord in Holy Communion. Martha welcomes him under her roof initially, but very soon she is distracted by the material demands of providing hospitality. Jesus, however, teaches her that there is an even higher form of hospitality that must be practiced. There are not only physical needs to be met, but also spiritual needs. There is nothing wrong with Martha's providing for the physical needs of Christ, but there is a time for her to do this and also a time for her to show him hospitality by being spiritually receptive to him. In this particular passage Jesus no doubt has something important to reveal to her, but Martha is not open to receiving it because of her distractions. Sometimes our distractions can hinder us from listening to the Lord when he wants to speak to our hearts. This is a very common problem, which often affects us during Holy Communion.

When one considers the reality of Holy Communion, one realises that this should be the most solemn and recollected moment of our lives. The Lord of Lords and the King of Kings literally comes to give himself to us in the most powerful and intimate encounter we can have with God while we are still on this earth. We receive the Incarnate God into our very beings. Martha was truly privileged in welcoming Jesus into her home, but we have an even greater privilege in welcoming him into our mortal bodies, that he may reign forever in our hearts. In spite of the grandeur of this gift, the moment of Holy Communion is often the moment when we are most distracted. Between being preoccupied about our personal lives and distracted by what might be going on around us in the church we often waste this moment of extraordinary grace. As Jesus himself once said to Saint Faustina, he comes in Holy Communion in order to fill us with graces, but often we do not understand his love and ignore his Real Presence.[5]

---

[5] Faustina Kowalska, *The Diary: Divine Mercy in My Soul* (Stockbridge, Mass.: Marian Press, 2003), no. 1385.

The attitude of Mary in this passage teaches us the way in which we must relate to Christ when he comes to visit us in the Eucharist. Mary is going from strength to strength in her contemplation of Christ. She seems to be penetrating beyond appearances and perceiving something of the divine nature of the Lord. She sits at his feet and listens to his word, but her heart is starting to glimpse the fact that he is the Word, that he is the God-man. In Holy Communion we must have a discerning heart, and using the power of the mind we must penetrate behind the eucharistic veil and see that it is truly Jesus we are encountering.

Saint Paul wrote that many Christians were sick and dying because of the disrespectful way they received Holy Communion. As he put it, they failed to "discern the body" (1 Cor 11:29–30). How often we receive the Host without perceiving that it is the living presence of the Body of Christ. With every Holy Communion we must make loving contact with the Person we receive. One way to do so is to spend some time in silent thanksgiving after Holy Mass. Many saints would spend half an hour or in some cases a full hour in thanksgiving after Holy Communion. We should at least try to be attentive and discern the presence of the Body of Christ for the fifteen minutes in which he is really present within our flesh. To do this is to open oneself to receiving the most extraordinary spiritual gifts and graces. In studying the lives of the saints we see that it was very often during their time of thanksgiving after Mass that they experienced mystical ecstasies and received insights that changed the world. Saint Teresa of Avila, a master of the spiritual life, described the importance of doing a prolonged thanksgiving after Mass in her book *The Way of Perfection*. We would do well to let her advice sink deeply into our minds and transform our way of approaching the altar of the Lord. In speaking of Holy Communion she wrote of herself in the third person:

> The Lord had given this person such a lively faith that, when she heard people say they wished they had lived when Christ walked on this earth, she would smile to herself, for she knew that we have Him as truly with us in the Most Holy Sacrament as people had Him then, and wonder what more they could possibly want.
>
> I know, too, that for many years this person, though by no means perfect, always tried to strengthen her faith, when she communicated, by thinking that it was exactly as if she saw the Lord entering her house, with her own bodily eyes, for she believed in very truth that this Lord was entering her poor abode, and she ceased, as far as she could, to think of outward things, and went into her abode with Him. She tried to recollect her senses so that they might all become aware of this great blessing, or rather, so that they should not hinder the soul from becoming conscious of it. She imagined herself at His feet and wept with the Magdalene exactly as if she had seen Him with her bodily eyes in the Pharisee's house.
>
> For, unless we want to be foolish and to close our minds to facts, we cannot suppose that this is the work of the imagination, as it is when we think of the Lord on the Cross, or of other incidents of the Passion, and picture within ourselves how these things happened. This is something which is happening now; it is absolutely true; and we have no need to go and seek Him somewhere

a long way off. For we know that, until the accidents of bread have been consumed by our natural heat, the good Jesus is with us and we should [not lose so good an opportunity but should] come to Him. If, while He went about in the world, the sick were healed merely by touching His clothes, how can we doubt that He will work miracles when He is within us, if we have faith, or that He will give us what we ask of Him since He is in our house? His Majesty is not wont to offer us too little payment for His lodging if we treat Him well. . . .

. . . [Jesus] reveals Himself to those who He knows will profit by His presence; though unseen by bodily eyes, He has many ways of revealing Himself to the soul through deep inward emotions and by various other means. Delight to remain with Him; do not lose such an excellent time for talking with Him as the hour after Communion. Remember that this is a very profitable hour for the soul; if you spend it in the company of the good Jesus, you are doing Him a great service. Be very careful, then, daughters, not to lose it.[6]

If even one soul follows this advice from a doctor of the Church and generously spends time with Jesus in silent thanksgiving after Mass, then the Lord will put up with all of the sacrileges, outrages and indifferences with which he is offended; because this one soul makes his coming worthwhile. The time which follows Holy Communion is the one time that we can all be sure that we are called to be Mary not Martha!

---

[6] Teresa of Avila, *The Way of Perfection*, 34

Anxious and troubled?

Saint Luke tells us that Martha was "distracted with much serving", and the Greek word he uses for "distracted" gives the impression that she is being dragged around in different directions. She cannot focus on the presence of the Lord in her home because she has too many activities in mind. She is not in control of her activities but is being controlled by them. Then Jesus with his deep gaze into the heart reveals that her problem is more than her being overwhelmed by exterior busyness, it is also her being interiorly "anxious and troubled". She has allowed the complications of daily life to disturb the peace of her heart. The word for "troubled" was translated into Latin with the word *turbaris*, which means "disturbed" and which comes from the root word for "commotion" or "crowd" or "noisy mob". There are too many thoughts racing through her mind like a thousand different voices. It is from this word that we derive the English word "turbulence". Martha is mobbed by troubling thoughts, and thus her soul is like the turbulent sea, while the soul of Mary, renewed in Christ, is like a calm lake. Martha has too much interior noise to be able to have the virtue of attentiveness to Christ.

The word for "anxious" describes excessive worry about material things, a disposition that smothers the spiritual life. The word literally means that she thinks too much about many things unworthy of using up the energies of her mind, while the mind of Mary is fixed upon the one thing necessary. To worry is to think too much about what causes fear, usually some apprehension about the future. It is the word that Christ used when he cautioned against fixing our minds on earthly realities as opposed to heavenly ones. He said: "Therefore I tell you, do not be anxious about your life, what you shall eat or what you shall drink, nor about your body, what you shall put on. Is not life more than food, and the body more than clothing?" (Mt 6:25). We should do what we can to provide for the material needs of our loved ones and then trust in the providence of God to take care of the rest. Anxiety about all of this can express a lack of trust in God. It is entirely useless and adds nothing to help the situation. Once we have done our best we can do no more and should simply follow the advice of Saint Peter who says: "Cast all your anxieties on him, for he cares about you" (1 Pt 5:7). The more we trust in the faithfulness of God's providence to care for us in the future and then concentrate upon seeking his glory, the more he will intervene to bless our lives.

In addition to this kind of anxiety, which is an excessive preoccupation about material things, there is also the related problem of anxiety about the problems of the world and the potential dangers of human existence. We cannot be indifferent to the sorrows of the world, but we cannot let our fears become disproportionate and ruin our lives. As long as Jesus is still present in the Eucharist, we can come to him and unburden our hearts. If our faith in his presence is strong then eucharistic adoration will give us deep peace, and in the light of the eucharistic Sun our troubles will fade away like the morning mist. Some people are afflicted by anxiety about their relationship with God. They have never fully come to know the merciful

goodness of the Lord, and so they live in slavish fear of
his justice. Anxiety can be especially problematic when
it is caused by guilt over past sins and the fear of future
punishment at the Last Judgement. If we have confessed
our sins then our guilt is erased, and we can be at peace
before the Lord. In this passage, the once sinful Magdalene is teaching us the remedy to excessive fear of divine
justice, and it is contemplation of Christ. Jesus is the Incarnation of God, who is a mystery of infinite, merciful
Love. The more we meditate upon his personality and
words the more we come to know the truth about the
personality of God.

Jesus makes visible the invisible mystery of God's
mercy. In him, it is as though the pure, inaccessible light
that is the essence of God passes through a prism and
we can behold all the colours of the divine mystery. In
looking at the Person of Jesus we see the full spectrum of
divine beauties made clear. The incomprehensible power,
wisdom, justice, mercy, patience and love of God are all
made accessible to the contemplation of human minds.
In meditating on the Gospels we see that when sinners
come face-to-face with God Incarnate they are not afraid
to come into his presence. On the contrary, sinners would
gather around him in droves. The fifth and fifteenth chapters of the Gospel of Luke make abundantly clear that the
revelation of the personality and the face of God in Jesus
Christ instilled confident trust in the hearts of sinners.
The more we consider this truth in prayer, the more we
receive unshakeable hope in the mercy God has for us. If
we want to know God's mercy it is Jesus alone who reveals it. We should imitate Mary and spend time adoring

the eucharistic face of Jesus, while listening to his Word in prolonged silent meditation. This is not like reading any other book because the Word of God is alive and active. It acts upon our minds and transforms our way of thinking, bringing deep peace to the soul as well as sanctifying our desires.

Many of our problems come from our incorrect way of thinking. Very often a thought we hold in our minds can cause a deep wave of sadness to enter into our entire being. One negative thought is enough to disturb us for many hours. In addition to causing this problem, our incorrect way of thinking is at the root of many of our sinful tendencies. An incorrect understanding of life can lead to actions that are contrary to the divine will. This is why when Jesus told his apostles to go out and make disciples (Mt 28:19), he used the Greek word for "conversion", *metanoia*, which connotes a transformation of one's way of thinking, which leads to a new Christian way of acting (Lk 24:47). Even for those of us who have had a true experience of conversion to the Lord, our way of thinking is not always entirely correct. Thankfully our thought processes can gradually be healed and elevated by meditation of the Word of God. Much time spent in meditation can correct our way of thinking about God, life and creation, and thus sanctify our desires and our entire lives.

Thoughts of material things do not merit the constant preoccupation of our minds, but thinking about the mysteries and the words of Jesus Christ is perhaps the noblest activity of the intellect. Truth, which is ultimately a Divine Person, is the proper object of the human mind, and it is the only object that brings the mind to fulfilment and peace. We are created to contemplate Truth for all eternity, and the more we do that here below the more we already begin to know the beginning of heavenly peace. We must learn to replace our troubling thoughts about many things with thoughts about Christ.

Martha worries about many useless things, but Mary has begun to think of almost nothing but Jesus and his teachings. Jesus says Martha is anxious and troubled, in that order. It is her anxious thinking about many things that invariably leads to trouble in the heart. Mary, on the other hand, fills her thoughts with the words of Christ, and this invariably leads to peace in the heart. As the prophet Isaiah says to the Lord: "You keep him in perfect peace, whose mind is stayed on you, because he trusts in you" (Is 26:3). It would be good to ask ourselves the following question: Of the 1,440 minutes in a day, how many of them do I spend thinking about Jesus and how many do I spend thinking of material things that are destined to pass away?

"Tell her to help me then!"

In the Greek text, Martha tells Jesus to command Mary "to join her in helping". The word that is used for "joining to help" is unusual. In this exact form the only other time it occurs is in Romans 8:26, where it speaks of the Spirit joining himself to us in our weakness and coming to our assistance from within to help us to pray. It is as though Martha wants Mary to unite herself to her very person, to her way of acting and thinking. Martha may be attached to Mary in a disordered way and is desiring that Mary join herself to her and be like her, to be as active and anxious about material things as she is.

In family circles, sometimes there are members who try to possess others. When someone seeks to spend more time with Christ in prayer, the family members with this problem may get annoyed and try to force the person to spend time with them instead. This is not true communion but disorder; true communion comes when each person is doing what he is supposed to be doing before God and with love. The one who receives the insight about how to do the divine will may often have to suffer at the hands of those who are guided only by their own wills. Part of the reason Mary broke away from Bethany in the first place may have been a desire to gain independence from her controlling older sister. Martha would one day be a great saint, but like Mary and like us all, she needed first to overcome her own sinful tendencies.

Disordered attachments can cause havoc, especially in families where there is no faith and when one person converts to Christianity. Family members may resent the convert's newfound happiness and different way of life, and jealousies may arise. People generally get attached to what they have always experienced and understood. Sudden changes in behaviour on the part of a converted relative can cause anxiety. Often converts have to suffer much in order to break free from the domination of others and live for Christ alone. A classic example of converts suffering from the reactions of their family members is found in the lives of Saints Francis and Clare of Assisi.

Although converts are often criticised by their relatives, as in the case of Mary and Martha, Jesus will always defend the one trying to come to him.

In families there should be total freedom of conscience to follow the will of God and to adopt the spiritual life that love for him inspires. It is important to note, however, that the relationship between a husband and a wife is unique, and a spouse's spiritual life must always respect the holy bond of marriage. Spiritual and religious activities must not be used as excuses for not spending time with one's spouse and children. This is why doctors of prayer (such as Saint Teresa of Avila) caution inexperienced priests against causing tensions in marriages through imprudent spiritual direction.

Young people must be helped to understand the importance of choosing the right vocation. An overriding desire to spend prolonged periods in prayer each day may well be a sign that a person is called to celibacy. This is what Saint Paul is warning us about in his letter to the Corinthians, where he says that an unmarried and devout person might find it easier to live for the Lord alone. Interestingly the word used to describe Martha's anxiety is the same as the one Saint Paul uses when speaking of the spiritual freedom that comes from celibacy. He says: "And the unmarried woman or virgin is anxious about the affairs of the Lord, how to be holy in body and spirit; but the married woman is anxious about worldly affairs, how to please her husband" (1 Cor 7:34).

The celibate state of life, especially when it is accompanied by a strong contemplative dimension, makes present in the world a foretaste of the eternal state of heavenly life, a life of perpetual adoration and unceasing contemplation of the face of God. When Jesus said that Mary had chosen the good "part" or "portion", we are reminded of what the Lord said to the Levites in the Old Testament (Num 18:20). They were not to inherit any specific part of the promised land because the Lord himself was to be their portion and their inheritance. The celibate person is not to be concerned about worldly possessions and lands because the presence of the Lord himself is to be his portion and inheritance. Such a person has a special right to live in a privileged state of intimacy with the eucharistic heart of Jesus. The choice for celibacy brings with it the freedom to spend much time with Christ in daily prayer.

To conclude, we can see in the Gospels that Saint Mary Magdalene has something to say to all Christians and that the texts in which she appears contain deep hidden mysteries, all of which are designed to enflame our hearts with love for Christ. The unforgettable fire of Mary's love never ceases to enkindle, or at least to fan, the flame of love in every generation of the Church's life on earth. Her mission is to spread her contagious brand of radical love for Christ to the ends of the earth.

∼

4

A Love Stronger than Death

After his visit to the house of Martha and Mary in Bethany, the Lord Jesus crossed over the Mount of Olives and continued his pilgrimage to the temple of Jerusalem for the feast of the Dedication. In these cold winter months, in the final year of his short life, he taught at length in the temple. In this place his teaching was different from that in Galilee, where his language was simpler and he seemed to adapt his words to the rural mentality of his audience, as in his use of parables (for example, see the parable of the sower in Lk 8:5). But in Jerusalem, amidst the doctors of the Law and the Scripture experts, he opened up deeper levels of the mysteries he had come to reveal to the world. For those who had the patience and the openness to ponder his message, rather than just pick out apparently controversial statements, he was explaining how the rituals of worship, in place since the days of Moses and David, were all preparing the way for what he had come to bestow upon them (Jn 7:37–38). The temple rituals had almost run their course, for the glorious reality had finally arrived (Jn 8:12). Above all, in Jerusalem he unveiled the mystery of his own divine identity (Jn 10:30).

After much debate in the holy city, it was his hints at his divine nature that were seized upon and definitively rejected, not by the ordinary sons and daughters of Abraham, but by the corrupt and powerful temple authorities. They knew that, if accepted, the implications of his message would completely transform the status quo and revolutionise the faith and worship of all of Israel. In spite of his signs and wonders, this was a prospect too disturbing to consider, especially for those who profited the most from the business of religion. Their attachment to long-held positions of power and the benefits that went with them was stronger than their openness to the will of God. Caiaphas, the high priest, did not care how wise Jesus was, he was a threat to his position and the order of things in Jerusalem and so was not to be tolerated. The chief priests and the Pharisees were freely choosing to blind themselves to the light of his truth (Jn 9:40–41), for in blindness there was the comfort of familiarity. If they were to accept Jesus' words as true, their own future status in Israel would be uncertain. Those who are set in their ways and attached to their privileges refuse to listen to any message that might bring an unsettling change.

The attitude towards Jesus among the Jerusalem elite became even colder than the winter weather. Not only were the authorities wary of the institutional upheaval his message would bring, but they were also bitterly envious of the reaction to his words among the simple faithful (Mk 15:10). His way of speaking was so sublime and his demeanour so majestic, that their own teaching and pomp seemed empty and vain. Envy is among the deadliest of sins because if it is left unchecked it will produce resentment, which can eventually turn into bitter hatred as it did in the case of Cain (Gen 4:1–16). During one of the times Christ was teaching, in their fanatical rage the authorities tried to have him stoned (Jn 10:31). After this clear manifestation of their rejection of his message, Jesus eventually decided to withdraw once again from the city that kills the prophets and stones those sent by God (Mt 23:37) and to make his way back to Perea (Jn 10:40).

It was there, beyond the river Jordan, in or around the month of February, that the news was brought to him that his friend Lazarus of Bethany was extremely ill. Since the conversion of his sister, Lazarus had become a friend and benefactor of Christ and his apostles. This explains the poignant message sent from his two sisters, Martha and Mary, reminding Jesus of how much he loved this dying man:

> Now a certain man was ill, Lazarus of Bethany, the village of Mary and her sister Martha. It was Mary who anointed the Lord with ointment and wiped his feet with her hair, whose brother Lazarus was ill. So the sisters sent to him, saying, "Lord, he whom you love is ill." But when Jesus heard it he said, "This illness is not unto death; it is for the glory of God, so that the Son of God may be glorified by means of it." (Jn 11:1–4)

Intercession and trust

In this introduction to the eleventh chapter of his Gospel, Saint John provides us with some very important details about the family of Bethany. The manner in which Lazarus is introduced here is very mysterious, and it seems that first of all John wants to situate Lazarus in relation to the well-known Lucan story about Martha and Mary. To mention Martha and Mary, as though they are well known, can only be a reference to the tenth chapter of the Gospel of Luke because John has not mentioned them before. He is not only clarifying the identity of Lazarus, who had not been mentioned by Luke in that story, as well as giving us the name of the village of Bethany, which was not given by Luke either; but he is also identifying Lazarus' sister Mary with the sinful woman who had anointed Christ's feet in Galilee (11:2). As mentioned earlier, the verb used by John indicates that he is speaking of a past event. The unusual style of this introduction, in which he first presents Lazarus and the two sisters and then goes back to clarify that Mary was actually the sister of Lazarus, further reminds us that Scripture's way of explaining things is not always the same as that of modern scholarship. A surface reading of biblical texts is never enough to grasp divine truths, and often it is a surface reading of things that has led to the rejection of the identification theory.

Returning to the intercession of the sisters for their brother, we note that the two worried sisters do not tell Jesus what he must do but simply appeal to his goodness and in this way offer us an example of how to intercede for the people we care about: "Lord, he whom you love is ill." Although the sisters do not explicitly ask Jesus to return to Bethany, where his life would be at risk, they still trust that his omnipotence will find a way of helping a man who they believe is too young to die. Deep down they have a secret desire that Jesus come in person and heal their brother (Jn 11:21), but they are reluctant to express a desire that might make Jesus feel obliged to put his life in peril once again. They have seen Jesus perform miracles for people he had never even met beforehand, and so it is to be reasonably expected that he will at least do something for his dearest friends. In the past he had healed people from afar just by willing it (Jn 4:50). To him all things are possible!

The fact that Lazarus is described here as one whom Jesus loves, and a little later on as a friend of Jesus and the apostles (Jn 11:11), even though he is never mentioned by the synoptic evangelists, adds to the deliberate sense of vagueness surrounding this family in the first three Gospels. How could the synoptic gospels fail to mention such a beloved disciple and friend of Christ, unless they did so for other reasons? They seem to have been obliged to be discreet about the family of Bethany, but John is by now free to reveal a little more about these dear friends of Christ. In any case, Jesus responds to the news by saying that this illness is not "unto death", or as we might alternatively translate it, "not going to end in death" (Jn 11:4). Surely this proclamation on the part of Christ, that Lazarus would not die, would have been immediately brought back to the sisters by the messengers, increasing their hope that Jesus would do something wonderful. How eagerly they were waiting to see his face, but John follows upon this introduction with a piece of Scripture that can only make us marvel at the unfathomable logic of the Lord: "Now Jesus loved Martha and her sister and Lazarus. So when he heard that he was ill, he stayed two days longer in the place where he was" (11:5-6).

The logic of the Cross

One would expect that the first part of the fifth verse would be followed by a statement explaining how Jesus immediately rushed off to Bethany to help his beloved friends. John seems almost to imply that the trial which Jesus allows to come upon his friends is motivated by how much he loves them! Intimacy with Christ does not spare a soul from trials. Even though Jesus does share choice "splinters of his Cross" with the souls closest to his heart, however, he also shares with them the most intense heavenly joys and consolations. Only when this story is over are we able to understand the goodness behind the Lord's way of acting. His friends in Bethany did not regret a minute of their suffering. Similarly, only when our lives are over do we fully understand the goodness of God and the spiritual value of our trials. Only when a grain of wheat falls to the ground and dies is it moving towards the most powerful and beautiful moment of its existence. Through the darkness of their trials the Lord brings his friends to the joy that surpasses all they hope for, and in the moment of darkness all he wants is their trust. Thus is the trust of Martha and Mary in the love of the Lord for them pushed to the limit. Not until the time is right for God to be glorified does Jesus decide to return to Bethany.

> Then after this he said to the disciples, "Let us go into Judea again." The disciples said to him, "Rabbi, the Jews were but now seeking to stone you, and are you going there again?" Jesus answered, "Are there not twelve hours in the day? If any one walks in the day, he does not stumble, because he sees the light of this world. But if any one

walks in the night, he stumbles, because the light is not in him." Thus he spoke, and then he said to them, "Our friend Lazarus has fallen asleep, but I go to awake him out of sleep." The disciples said to him, "Lord, if he has fallen asleep, he will recover." Now Jesus had spoken of his death, but they thought that he meant taking rest in sleep. Then Jesus told them plainly, "Lazarus is dead; and for your sake I am glad that I was not there, so that you may believe. But let us go to him." Thomas, called the Twin, said to his fellow disciples, "Let us also go, that we may die with him" (Jn 11:7-16).

Expectations surpassed

Our Lord had promised that the sickness of Lazarus would not end in death and only two days later he tells his apostles that Lazarus is dead. The word of Christ is mysteriously profound. Although at times it may seem that his promises have failed, in reality his word is always realised. He promised that the gates of hell would not prevail against the Church (Mt 16:18), but at times we are tempted to think that they are indeed prevailing. Jesus demands heroic trust from his friends, and this means that he demands a trust that remains intact even when the appearance of things tempts us to think that our trust is in vain. Saints continue to trust, even in the most apparently impossible situations, and it is such trust that is demanded of Martha and Mary. We can imagine how confused they must have been in front of all the crowds of mourners who knew of their closeness to the Miracle Worker, who seemingly had abandoned them in their hour of greatest need. They needed to learn to accept that God's ways are not our ways but that he often does much more than we can even hope for.

We see a pattern in the life of Mary Magdalene, and perhaps it can be seen in the life of all of Christ's faithful adorers. In her life there is a cycle that repeats itself and culminates in the eternal joy of heaven. She desired happiness and earnestly sought it, but her desires were left unfulfilled or disappointed, only to be surpassed and fulfilled to a higher degree than she had initially desired. First she sought happiness in the world and in the love of sinful creatures, but this left her with only darkness and emptiness until the day Jesus arrived and introduced her to divine love and happiness infinitely deeper than that which other poor sinners can give. She discovered that she had actually been seeking too little happiness. She had been seeking to satisfy her thirst for infinite love in ways that left her more unfulfilled, but in the encounter with Jesus, true infinite love flooded her soul and from that moment onwards she could never look back to the things she had left behind.

In the illness of Lazarus we see a similar pattern. Mary desperately desired for Jesus to come and heal her brother, but this desire was frustrated as her dear brother took his last breath in her arms. Yet again she had desired something far less extraordinary than Jesus had planned to bestow. Her family was chosen to receive one of the greatest miracles in human history. For love of her and her family and to glorify the power of God, Jesus reversed the natural laws of creation and raised her brother to life, four days after his death. Again we observe that she had desired something and was left bitterly disappointed, but then Jesus gave her much more than she initially desired. Later on, we will see that this pattern will repeat itself once again in an even more extraordinary manner! Let us behold the solemn moment of Christ's eventual arrival in Bethany:

> Now when Jesus came, he found that Lazarus had already been in the tomb four days. Bethany was near Jerusalem, about two miles off, and many of the Jews had come to Martha and Mary to console them concerning their brother. When Martha heard that Jesus was coming, she went and met him, while Mary sat in the house. Martha said to Jesus, "Lord, if you had been here, my brother would not have died. And even now I know that whatever you ask from God, God will give you." Jesus said to her, "Your brother will rise again." Martha said to him, "I know that he will rise again in the resurrection at the last day." Jesus said to her, "I am the resurrection and the life; he who believes in me, though he die, yet shall he live, and whoever lives and believes in me shall never die. Do you believe this?" She said to him, "Yes, Lord; I believe that you are the Christ, the Son of God, he who is coming into the world."
>
> When she had said this, she went and called her sister Mary, saying quietly, "The Teacher is here and is calling for you." And when she heard it, she rose quickly and went to him. Now Jesus had not yet come to the village, but was still in the place where Martha had met him. When the Jews who were with her in the house, consoling her, saw Mary rise quickly and go out, they followed her, supposing that she was going to the tomb to weep there. Then Mary, when she came where Jesus was and saw him, fell at his feet, saying to him, "Lord,

if you had been here, my brother would not have died."
(Jn 11:17–32)

Mary and Martha were devastated by the loss of their brother and by the fact that Jesus had not come to help them. They must have asked themselves a thousand times why the Lord let their brother die. Trying to make sense of the mystery of death, they would have been tempted by the usual falsehoods that almost always well up in a grief-stricken soul. First, they would have tried to find some way of blaming themselves for what had happened, then other people, and then perhaps the physician who could have done more to help their brother. Then they would have been tempted to think that perhaps poor Lazarus himself had done something to merit his premature end. Above all they would have been tempted by that most dangerous of all temptations, the one which the accuser will invariably try to whisper into the aching human heart at some point or another, namely, the temptation to doubt the love of the Lord.

Original sin has given us a false idea of God, and because sin brought suffering in its wake, people are always tempted to rebel against the Lord in the hour of darkness. On one hand this family had experienced deeply the love of God manifested in Jesus Christ and could even call Lazarus with certainty "the one whom Jesus loved"; but in the hour of darkness even the memory of the consolations we have received from the goodness of the Lord tend to hide themselves, and it is then that the devil tries to make us rebel and blaspheme the good God. As in the case of holy Job, the spirit of the world tells us to look at our sufferings and then "curse God and die!" (Job 2:9). Did the sisters yield to this temptation to blame Jesus or did they continue to trust in his goodness? We can only speculate as to the answer. It is hard to imagine one as sincere and radical in her love for Jesus as Mary Magdalene, ever falling into the trap of doubting the goodness of the Lord.

In any case, as soon as the sisters finally see the Lord before them, they both say the same thing, namely, that if Jesus had been present Lazarus would be alive (Jn 11:21, 32). This spontaneous statement reveals what must have been the subject of their conversation and the dominant thought in their minds. It is interesting to note that nowhere in the Gospels does anybody die when the Prince of Life is present. Furthermore, every time Jesus comes in contact with a dead body he raises it to life. All of this gives us a little glimpse of what will happen on the Last Day, when he will call the dead from their tombs. The sisters knew this and felt that it was unnecessary for their brother to die when Jesus could have come and saved him. They are essentially showing their frustration with life and death in this valley of tears. Now comes something unexpected and beautiful beyond imagining. The tears of Martha had drawn from the heart of Jesus an enlightening discourse on the identity of the Christ, as well as grounds for hope in the face of death and sorrow. The tears of Mary will bring about something far greater.

> When Jesus saw her weeping, and the Jews who came with her also weeping, he was deeply moved in spirit and troubled; and he said, "Where have you laid him?" They

said to him, "Lord, come and see." Jesus wept. So the Jews said, "See how he loved him!" But some of them said, "Could not he who opened the eyes of the blind man have kept this man from dying?" Then Jesus, deeply moved again, came to the tomb; it was a cave, and a stone lay upon it. (Jn 11:33–38)

Tears from heaven

Jesus wept! This is the shortest and most touching line in Scripture. Jesus, who reveals to us the invisible mystery of God, shed tears when he saw the sorrow of his beloved friend. This shows not only that the Lord in his divine beatitude is not indifferent to our sorrow but that Christ is a man! He is truly and fully human, and in his human nature there dwells a most compassionate heart. By her gestures of adoration Magdalene teaches us something about his divinity, but here through her tears she has obtained for us the greatest manifestation of his humanity.

In the humanity of Christ we admire the synthesis all of the human perfections and virtues at work. He is the strongest of men, defying the murderous authorities of Jerusalem and making war on the powers of hell itself; and at the same time he is the gentlest of men, going so far as to shed tears in public. A man does not weep easily in front of a crowd, especially a man who is surrounded by enemies seeking to know his weak points. A man is afraid to shed tears because doing so shows weakness or vulnerability, and a man showing weakness is like a soldier laying down his arms in the midst of battle. Yet here

Jesus is profoundly moved by his friend Mary's tears and so he simply weeps. He is too free to be concerned about narrow human opinions of him. He never lets himself be governed by what sinful men expect of him, nor influenced in his actions by pressure coming from his enemies.[1]

Every action of Jesus is done to please God the Father and to love the person before him. He is the perfect man, filled with the gentle but invincible power that comes from perfect love. And now he reveals that he is more than a man, that even the greatest of men the world has ever known cannot be put into the same category with him. In him there is a power that this world has never seen before or again and here human history catches a glimpse of that power which will be fully unleashed only at the end of time:

> Jesus said, "Take away the stone." Martha, the sister of the dead man, said to him, "Lord, by this time there will be an odor, for he has been dead four days." Jesus said to her, "Did I not tell you that if you would believe you would see the glory of God?" So they took away the stone. And Jesus lifted up his eyes and said, "Father, I thank you that you have heard me. I knew that you always hear me, but I have said this on account of the people standing by, that they may believe that you sent me." When he had said this, he cried with a loud voice, "Lazarus, come out." The dead man came out, his hands and feet bound with bandages, and his face wrapped with a cloth. Jesus said to them, "Unbind him, and let him go." (Jn 11:39–44)

[1] Raymond Léopold Bruckberger, O.P., *Marie Madeleine* (Paris: La Jeune Parque, 1953), p. 102.

Scripture often clothes the most extraordinary events in the simplest of language, in the same way that the Holy Spirit once clothed the glorious Eternal Word in the humility of our flesh. It is marvellous to see the wonders of the Incarnation, the institution of the Eucharist, the Passion and the Resurrection all described in very simple words, often with no great build-up or dramatic introduction. The words of God do not always follow the same literary logic as the words of man, and here the Gospel text describes the most stunning of events with the plainest of words. The resurrection of Lazarus was a moment that amazed the whole of Judaea, and to the dismay of the Pharisees, the news of it might have soon convinced the whole nation that the Messiah had arrived; yet it is described by John in a very matter-of-fact manner. We should not let the subtle use of language make us underestimate the importance of this event. Yes, Elijah had once raised somebody from the dead by his prayers (1 Kings 17:17–22), but to raise a man from the dead four days after he had died was unthinkable.

Jesus had earlier said that he rejoiced to do this sign because it would bring his disciples to deeper faith (Jn 11:14–15). It was the super-sign that brought Jerusalem to a definitive moment of decision. The authorities had to pronounce judgement; either recognise the evidence before their eyes and announce the arrival of the Messiah or else continue to claim that Jesus of Nazareth was some kind of malevolent wonder-worker, under the influence of the devil, and a blasphemer to be rejected. This latter argument was now growing weaker and weaker, since everybody knew that a demoniac could not possibly do what Jesus had just done. Even a few of the Pharisees were starting to say that he must have heaven on his side if he can do such things (Jn 9:16).

There were too many eye-witnesses present at the resurrection of Lazarus for the religious leaders to deny that this man had worked a miracle of incomparable significance on the doorstep of Jerusalem itself. What would he not do next? They had already threatened him with stoning, and yet he had boldly returned to the region and his influence was growing out of control. The enemies of Christ had to act quickly. They knew that they would have to do everything in their power to curb the effect of this miracle and to put an end to the life of Jesus as soon as possible, before he had a chance to do anything further of this kind.

> Many of the Jews therefore, who had come with Mary and had seen what he did, believed in him; but some of them went to the Pharisees and told them what Jesus had done. So the chief priests and the Pharisees gathered the council, and said, "What are we to do? For this man performs many signs. If we let him go on like this, everyone will believe in him, and the Romans will come and destroy both our holy place and our nation." But one of them, Caiaphas, who was high priest that year, said to them, "You know nothing at all; you do not understand that it is expedient for you that one man should die for the people, and that the whole nation should not perish." He did not say this of his own accord, but being high priest that year he prophesied that Jesus should die for the nation, and not for the nation only, but to gather into one the children of God who are scattered abroad. So from that day on they took counsel about how to put him to death (Jn 11:45–53).

Their last chance for rallying support was to invoke the need to protect the temple, the glory of all of Israel, as a pretext for eliminating the unpredictable Galilean. They needed to find some way of frightening the people into believing that his ministry would provoke the wrath of the Romans. With the temple destroyed, God's magnificent dwelling place would be gone from the land, and this was a terrifying thought for everybody.

Unbeknownst to the chief priests who argued in this way, they were in reality forcing the rest of the Sanhedrin into making a choice between two temples (Jn 2:21). Jesus himself was the new Temple, the place of God's Real Presence on earth. The body of Jesus was the Temple designed by God the Father and his Holy Spirit, and with his arrival in the world, the temple that had been constructed by human hands was destined to pass away before long. As Mary Magdalene instinctively adored the sacred body of Jesus, she was a visible personification of the response that God expected from all mankind. She would not be swayed by the sophistry of the chief priests and the religious experts of Jerusalem. She had chosen the true and lasting Temple. Her heart had found that for which it was created and the contentment for which it longed in adoration of the Divine Person of Jesus Christ.

Looking with love at the eucharistic face of Jesus is the closest thing on earth to the ecstatic gaze of the beatific vision. In the body of Christ, the thrice-holy God has made himself capable of being looked upon by sinners here on earth. Original and actual sin had darkened our intellects and made us incapable of seeing God with the spiritual vision of the mind. Spiritually we had become like some poor man who has lived in a dark cave for a long time and who cannot immediately walk out into the noonday sunlight. He has to grow accustomed to looking at the light once again. Our minds have to grow accustomed to beholding the light of God so that we can walk out into the blaze of his glory when we die; and this entails being purified through contemplation. Worship of the sacred humanity of the Eternal Word, Jesus Christ, is the remedy for our spiritual vision that God our Father has prepared for us. His flesh, which was like our own, taken from the dust of the earth, is like the healing remedy applied to the eyes of the blind man in the Gospel (Jn 9:6–7). The more we behold the divine light, gently revealed through his humanity, the more we are given back our mystical vision. Even without having passed through the purifications necessary before we will finally be able to look upon God's glory in an unmediated way, in Jesus we have already begun to see God. In adoring the holy face of Jesus, which was transfigured and shone like the sun on Mount Tabor, it is as though we can stare at the divine Sun with our sinful eyes and not go blind! In this contemplative gaze upon Christ, we are gently and joyfully prepared for the day when we will see the divine essence fully unveiled in heaven. This is the joy of the new Temple, which God the Father bestowed upon the world in giving us the sacred Body of Christ. This is the joy of eucharistic adoration!

As a result of this astounding miracle in Bethany, the authorities also began to discuss the possible execution of innocent Lazarus (Jn 12:10–11) in spite of his popularity and the respect he commanded in Judaea. His testimony would forever be a nuisance to them, and innocent though he was, bearing witness to Jesus Christ was a crime worthy of death as far as they were concerned. Desperate times call for desperate measures, and they were prepared to do anything to prevent people from believing that Jesus was the Christ. Aware of the plot against him and aware that his hour had not yet come, Jesus "no longer went about openly among the Jews, but went from there to the country near the wilderness, to a town called Ephraim; and there he stayed with the disciples" (Jn 11:54). There Jesus could pray in silence and spend some final precious moments forming the hearts of his apostles in peace.

The power of Love

The miraculous resurrection of Lazarus seems to have been called forth from the compassionate heart of Jesus, above all by the tears of his beloved Magdalene. This is the kind of wonder Jesus works for the hearts that love him deeply. Today, in the Eucharist, this awesome power of Christ remains present in the world, and at times he manifests a little glimpse of it. Saint Dominic is said to have raised a dead man to life by the celebration of Holy Mass and the shedding of many tears before the eucharistic face of Jesus. Our Lord sometimes works these wonders of the physical order as signs, but at all times he is working wonders in the supernatural order.

Several decades ago, in the city of Paris, the eucharistic Lord brought about the marvellous spiritual resurrection of a famous atheistic journalist named André Frossard. He had grown up in a communist family and had no belief whatsoever in the existence of God. Then one day he entered a chapel of perpetual eucharistic adoration, looking for a friend, whom he had seen entering there. He had no idea what kind of a chapel it was, and as he walked in and glanced towards the altar he noticed a group of people all kneeling around what seemed to him to be a "golden object with a white circle in the middle" surrounded by candles. In the moment he looked towards the monstrance, he heard an interior voice whisper, "spiritual life". Instantly he received an intellectual infusion of the mysteries of the holy Catholic Faith. He not only believed all of what we believe, but he also received a grace to penetrate and understand deep divine mysteries.[2] The Holy Spirit transformed his interior life in a marvellous manner. He continued to write for one of the most well-known French newspapers, *Le Figaro*, and he became one of the strongest voices of Christian truth in twentieth-century France. Through his writings, the light of the Faith continued to shine in difficult days for the Church in that country, and all of it dated back to the moment in which a ray of eucharistic power raised him from spiritual death to the fullness of life.

The prayers of the faithful souls in the presence of the Blessed Sacrament day and night in that chapel bore the most extraordinary fruit in the conversion of this great man of God.

From the silence of his eucharistic dwelling place, Jesus is "working still" (Jn 5:17), but his work is usually

---

[2] André Frossard, *Dieu existe, je l'ai rencontré* (Paris: Fayard, 1976), pp. 103–10.

brought about because of the prayers of a loving heart that knows how to remain in his presence and intercede for the world. Jesus can work wonders independent of us but wants us to share in his causal power, and this is why he often makes certain graces dependent upon our intercession. All over the world stories are told of the conversions or spiritual resurrections that adorers obtain from the eucharistic heart of Jesus. Wherever there is a spiritual Lazarus raised from the dead, very often there is a weeping Magdalene who has brought it about. We see this in the lives of Saints Augustine and Monica, as well as in countless others down through the centuries.

∼

5

The Passion Prophesied

A few weeks after the resurrection of Lazarus, and little more than one week before his own death, Jesus took leave of the quiet town of Ephraim, where he had spent a good part of the month of March. The magnificent flowers of springtime were by now almost in full bloom all around them, and the twelve apostles were grateful to have spent some time in peace at the feet of the Master. But now Jesus told them to prepare themselves for the pilgrimage to Jerusalem for the feast of Passover. Trepidation seized the hearts of the apostles, who were fully aware of the dangers involved in such a journey, not only for Jesus, but also for themselves as his followers. The Lord assured them, however, that this was the will of the Father and that was all that mattered.

Passing by way of Jericho (Lk 19:1), he and his apostles eventually arrived back in Bethany, where they would rest before entering the holy city. Upon arrival in the village, Jesus was warmly welcomed by its inhabitants. The same fervour that Christ had known in the early days of his public ministry in Capernaum met him in this village, and a large banquet was prepared for him in the house of Simon the leper, whom he had healed some time before.

It was here that Mary Magdalene would anoint Christ's feet a second time and in an even more extravagant manner than the earlier anointing in Galilee. At first glance there appears to be a slight discrepancy in the chronology of the second anointing in the different Gospels. Looking closer, however, we see that rather than provide a precise chronological account of this anointing, the synoptic gospels show us that there is a link between what happens at the banquet in Bethany and the decision of Judas to betray Christ to those who were seeking to kill him. They knew he would arrive in the holy city for the feast of Passover, but they also knew that the place would be teeming with rowdy Galileans, many of whom still counted Jesus as a prophet and who would be capable of causing a riot if he were arrested in public (Mk 14:1–2). In spite of the urgent need to eliminate Jesus as soon as possible, the chief priests were prepared to wait until things had calmed down after the Passover; until suddenly there appeared in their midst a disgruntled disciple of Christ himself, finally driven to the madness of betraying his own Master after what he had just experienced in Bethany. Thus it is important to meditate deeply on what happened at the fateful banquet that is part of the background for the celebration of Holy Week.

The precious perfume of love

John tells us that Jesus arrived in Bethany six days before the Passover, and it would seem that the banquet was organised for him shortly after his arrival. We can presume it happened on the evening before Christ's triumphant entry into Jerusalem. While the synoptic evangelists show us the event as a kingly anointing of Christ's head before he takes possession of his kingdom through his Passion and death, John is anxious to remind us that it was an anointing not only of his head but also of his feet. Here are the details that John wanted history not to forget:

> Six days before the Passover, Jesus came to Bethany, where Lazarus was, whom Jesus had raised from the dead. There they made him a supper; Martha served, and Lazarus was one of those at table with him. Mary took a pound of costly ointment of pure nard and anointed the feet of Jesus and wiped his feet with her hair; and the house was filled with the fragrance of the ointment. But Judas Iscariot, one of his disciples (he who was to betray him), said, "Why was this ointment not sold for three hundred denarii and given to the poor?" This he said, not that he cared for the poor but because he was a thief, and as he had the money box he used to take what was put into it. Jesus said, "Let her alone, let her keep it for the day of my burial. The poor you always have with you, but you do not always have me."
>
> When the great crowd of the Jews learned that he was there, they came, not only on account of Jesus but also to see Lazarus, whom he had raised from the dead. So the chief priests planned to put Lazarus also to death, because on account of him many of the Jews were going away and believing in Jesus. (Jn 12:1–11)

Commentators sometimes ask if this precious ointment had perhaps been left over from the burial of wealthy Lazarus and was now being used by his sister as a gesture of gratitude for his resurrection. It may alternatively have been the last jar of precious perfume left over from Mary's former life; or it may be that she felt prompted to buy it especially for Jesus. Of these possibilities we cannot be certain, but thanks to the greed and outrage of Judas, we do know that the ointment or perfumed oil that Mary used here was extraordinarily valuable. It was worth a year's salary. Today we would be talking about thousands and thousands of dollars-worth of the rarest and most precious perfume in the world, spilled out in an instant. It was made of pure unadulterated spikenard and, to preserve its potency, kept in an air-tight alabaster jar. Sometimes a jar of this kind would be smashed in the tomb of a deceased loved one at the moment of burial. Such rare and costly perfume would have been imported to the markets of Jerusalem from somewhere in the East.

John highlights for us the exceptionally generous character of this anointing and clarifies that it was accomplished by "Mary of Bethany", something the synoptic evangelists do not explain. It seems difficult to doubt that the woman who does this highly unusual thing is the sinful woman of the first anointing. Yet if not for John, we would never have known that the second anointing was done by Mary of Bethany. Surely Mark and Matthew were both familiar with Mary of Bethany and her well-known family, but they simply say that a woman anointed Jesus. Scripture is mysterious and we do not know why certain people's identities are at times not clearly explained. Thus we can see that the argument that Luke does not identify the sinner with Mary is insufficient for rejecting the identification theory.

Another silent prophecy

It is lovely to behold the silent audacity of the saint as she approaches the all-holy presence of Christ. She says nothing, for what she is doing is too sacred to be mixed with clumsy human words. She lets her love alone do the talking and once again it prophesies. Through her gesture of love, God reveals to the world that the hour of redemption has arrived. The immaculate flesh of the Lamb without stain will soon be pierced through for our sins. It is Jesus alone who can interpret this prophecy that brings such solemn tidings for human history.

What happened between them is what Saint Peter-Julian Eymard said is what happens in eucharistic adoration. It is the silent "dialogue of love" between the soul and Christ. It is a silent reciprocal gaze of love in which "deep calls to deep" (Ps 42:7), and a bond is being brought about between a human soul and a Divine Person with a human nature. Mary knows that she is constantly being judged by others, but understood by Christ, whose eyes behold the heart and not just appearances. As he sees her before him, Jesus knows that this beautiful soul is capable of understanding far more than so many others because she has learned the secret of love. She has learned from his Mother the sacred art of silently pondering the mystery of love that is Jesus Christ. There is a mutual understanding between deep souls and their Master. The Good Shepherd knows his sheep and his sheep know him. As the all-seeing gaze of Jesus penetrates the hearts of all in the supper room of Bethany, he sees many things that displease him. He sees worldliness, self-interest, even treachery, but there is one heart that is true and desires only to let him know how much his presence means to her. While others are busy chatting and filled with distractions, Jesus looks into the depths of Mary's heart and finds something of what he has found in the heart of his Mother; he finds attentiveness to his presence, the attentiveness of love. He finds adoration.

Some Church Fathers have found symbolism in the details given by the evangelists who recount this event. If we put the different descriptions of the perfume together we can say that Mary comes carrying a precious alabaster jar of pure or unadulterated, extremely costly, spikenard perfumed oil. The word that is used in Greek for "pure" or "unadulterated" could also be translated as "genuine", and its origin comes from the word for "faithful" or "trustworthy". The contents of this jar are symbolic of what Jesus sees when he looks into the heart of Magdalene. She is faithful and true! A thousand other disciples could be seduced into betraying Christ but never she! We have all met souls like this, whose love is too pure and too strong to betray their beloved. Her loving, loyal heart is symbolised by that precious perfume, and when she comes before the Lord her love is like a sweet sacrifice. It is like a draught of cold water to a divine heart that is parched with the thirst to be loved.

Christ has come into this world to reveal the love of God for souls and also the desire of God to be loved. As he has made known to the mystics through the ages, his final cry of "I thirst" was a revelation of God's infinite desire for our love. He has even gone so far as to explain that this consuming divine thirst remains ever present in the Blessed Sacrament where Christ waits perpetually for our presence and our love. In the heart of Magdalene, the Divine Lord found the kind of angelic love that is a glimpse of the life of heaven.

In the Middle Ages, the monastics in such famous abbeys as Le Barroux in France saw in Saint Mary Magdalene a model of man's response to divine love. They taught that if the perfume of love for God is to remain unadulterated, it must be surrounded by the air-tight alabaster jar of much silence. Too many distractions and worldly desires make our love for God evaporate, and as the life of Magdalene teaches us, it is only through the holy silence of contemplation of Christ that the perfume of love remains intact. She was the woman who did "something beautiful" for Christ, something worthy of eternal memory, because she was first the woman who sat in silence at his feet listening to his Word.

A living sacrifice of spiritual worship (Rom 12:1)

Magdalene was never one to care too much about what people thought of her; before her conversion this attitude appeared to others as a kind of selfish recklessness, but after her conversion this attitude was elevated by grace and became a precious virtue. Saints are characterised by the desire to please God in all of their actions. Some people never get far along the road to holiness because they are too attached to their reputations and afraid of what others will think if they do anything seemingly radical out of love for God. People can fail to do the will of God because through fear they are enslaved to doing what others expect from them. Magdalene's reckless freedom was transformed by Christ into a holy freedom to serve God alone.

In the anointing stories, we see Magdalene's holy recklessness. Although it was seriously frowned upon for a woman to undo her hair in public, she does so to show her love for Jesus. The whole world may think she is insane, but if Jesus is happy with her then she is happy. In the first anointing she had used her hair to dry the feet of Christ she had soaked with her tears; in the second one, she uses her hair to dry off the excess perfume with which she had drenched his holy feet. Even the apostles were probably made uncomfortable by the boundless liberty of this woman; however, Mary does not act to please them but Jesus Christ alone. To use her long hair, which had been the symbol of her beauty, in this humble way symbolises the offering of all that she is and all that is most precious to her as a living sacrifice to God. This is true adoration, to submit everything, even life itself, as a gift to God.

Some souls receive the special grace to offer themselves in a radical way from the very beginning of their relationship with Jesus. Blessed Charles de Foucauld was a great devotee of Saint Magdalene, and he would regularly visit her grotto in la Sainte Baume. He too had lived the wildest of lives and was converted when a priest practically forced him to go to confession. In the moment of absolution all of his doubts vanished and he knew with certitude that God existed. From that very instant he gave himself to the Lord in holy celibacy and wanted nothing but to live for

God alone. He said: "As soon as I believed that there was a God, I understood that I could not do otherwise than to live for Him alone."[1] Magdalene seems to have had a similar experience: from the moment of her conversion all she could do was offer herself entirely to God. From that moment, her money, her beauty, her very life, existed for Jesus alone. She had so powerfully united herself to the heart of Christ through love, that she would also be joined to his Passion and death, so as to share in the first fruits of his Resurrection on Easter Sunday morning.

The new Holy of Holies

In a previous chapter we spoke of the sacred Body of Christ as the new Temple for mankind. His flesh is the place where God truly dwells in this world. When Jesus spoke of his body as the new Temple in the Gospel of John, the word that he used was not the one that refers to the entire temple, with its different precincts, but the one that specifically refers to the inner sanctuary, what is called the Holy of Holies, the place where the presence of the Lord was to be found (Jn 2:19–21).

The history of this holy place goes back to the mountain of Sinai when Moses encountered God in the mysterious cloud and received instructions to construct the tabernacle, which was to have an inner part for the Ark of the Covenant. The Ark contained, among other things, some manna, the bread from heaven that fed the Israelites

[1] Charles de Foucauld, *Un Temps Avec Charles de Foucauld: 1858–1916*, ed. Philippe Baud (Paris: Éditions du Cerf, 1998), p. 7.

in the wilderness. In the outer part of the tabernacle was a table with the Bread of the Presence (Ex 25:23–30). Once the tabernacle was constructed, the holy cloud, which marked God's presence on earth, came and filled it, to confirm that God dwelled there in a special way (Ex 40:34). Eventually this holy dwelling place of God was transferred to the temple of Jerusalem, and during the consecration of the temple the awesome cloud returned to show that Jerusalem was now the place where God's glory dwelled upon the earth (1 Kings 8:10–11). This mysterious glory of God's presence became known as the *Shekinah*. The Jewish people loved to approach this place but at the same time they would have been terrified to draw too close to the Holy of Holies because of a sense of their own unworthiness before the majestic presence of God.

Jesus taught that the tabernacle God instructed Moses to build was a preparation for his coming into the world, when his sacred Body would become our true Holy of Holies. His Body is infinitely holier than any building, and yet through the mystery of the Incarnation he has allowed us to approach him without fear. From the moment that God took flesh in the womb of Mary and veiled his blinding glory, we have come to understand the full truth about his loving mercy. He is still the God of infinite holiness, but in his mercy he has made himself accessible to poor sinners. If we approach him with humility and sincerity we will never be turned away. In his magnificent sermon on the Bread of Life, Jesus comforted our fearful hearts with the following words of love: "All that the Father gives me will come to me; and him who comes to me I will not cast out. For I have come down from heaven, not to do my own will, but the will of him who sent me; and this is the will of him who sent me; that I should lose nothing of all that he has given me; but raise it up at the last day" (Jn 6:37–39).

Magdalene is so drawn by this loving warmth of the Sacred Heart that she forgets her own sinfulness and boldly approaches the Divine Lord to anoint him. It is interesting to note that in the Old Testament, there was an anointing of the priests, the prophets and the kings, and we can see Magdalene's anointing of Christ's head as a sign that his priestly, kingly and prophetic missions will soon be consummated in Jerusalem. There was also an anointing of the Holy of Holies itself in the Old Testament. In the same way we anoint our altars with holy oil today, the tabernacle with its contents was also anointed (Lev 8:10). Through Mary Magdalene the new Holy of Holies is anointed so as to become accessible to sinners through the Paschal Mystery.

Another interesting detail about the old Holy of Holies is that twice a day the priest would offer sweet-smelling incense on the table where the Bread of the Presence was to be found. The fragrant incense would fill the whole tabernacle, in much the same way as the sweet smell of spikenard perfume filled the whole house in Bethany. One of the ingredients of the sweet incense for the old Holy of Holies was spikenard.[2] In this anointing of the new Holy of Holies, a whole new order is being instituted. If we look at the gesture of Mary Magdalene in the

---

[2] *Talmud, Keritot* 6a.

light of that Old Testament prefiguration of the Body of Christ, the Holy Spirit is perhaps teaching us that what is really required is the sweet fragrance of our loving adoration in the Real Presence of the sacred Body of Jesus Christ.

The sacred body of Jesus is present in heaven at the right of the Father and on earth in the Most Holy Eucharist, which is the fulfilment of the Bread of the Presence in the tabernacle, beside which arose the sweet incense twice daily. Like Mary Magdalene we can now enter boldly into the holy place and rejoice in the presence of the One who welcomes us and desires us to be with him. His delight is to be in the presence of the sons of men (Prov 8:31). A humble, contrite heart filled with love for Jesus in the Eucharist is the sweet-smelling incense that all of the Old Testament was pointing towards.

When Jesus spoke of his body as the Temple, or the Holy of Holies, he spoke especially of his risen body (Jn 2:19). That risen body was not only destined to be our Holy of Holies for the forty days between the Resurrection and the Ascension. That risen body is with us always, until the end of time, in the Blessed Sacrament. All future generations were destined to come into contact with the risen body of Jesus through the Eucharist. Saint Thomas Aquinas said that Christ's head symbolises his divinity and his feet symbolise his humanity; when we adore both we accomplish today a mystical anointing of the Lord.[3] We must train our eyes to pierce through the eucharistic veil and gaze into the eyes of the God-man.

---

[3] Thomas Aquinas, *Commentary on the Gospel of John*, 1599.

To have seen him is to have seen the Eternal Father, and to gaze at him with love, truly present, in the flesh, in eucharistic adoration is to anoint not only his head but his feet too (Jn 14:9).

An antithesis of loves

The prophetess of love, Mary Magdalene, foretold by the anointing at Bethany the imminence of the Passion and death of the Lamb of God. She probably did not know why she did what she did; she simply followed the inspirations of love that welled up within her heart, and it is in this way that she came into union with the divine will. Jesus knew that within a few short days his body would be dead and buried. Christ would soon undergo the cruelest of tortures. The anticipation of this suffering had already begun to trouble the soul of Christ, but in Bethany, the love of Mary Magdalene was like a consoling balm to comfort him in his time of sorrow. In the first anointing, Mary's love was called upon to repair the Pharisee's neglect of Christ; in the second her love was called upon to repair a wound far more painful to the heart of Jesus. Magdalene's adoration of Christ often draws out what is hidden in the hearts of those who observe her. First it drew out the self-righteousness of a Pharisee, next the distracted anxiety of her overly active but sincere sister. At the anointing in Bethany it brought to the surface the poison that had remained hidden in the heart of Judas. Adoration and love for Jesus reveal the secret thoughts of many hearts.

The truth in the heart of Judas was that he opposed the ways of Christ. The spiritual and mysterious ways of Jesus bitterly disappointed him; Jesus of Nazareth failed to fulfil Judas' expectations of the Messiah. He wanted a strong man who would win over the crowds to his cause and lead them to retake Jerusalem from the Romans and gloriously restore the dynasty of David.

The closest that Jesus had come to seeming as if he might be able to accomplish such a thing was a year beforehand in Galilee, when he miraculously fed five thousand men who were willing to carry him to Jerusalem and enthrone him king of Israel. This was the beginning of a potential army gathering itself around the Lord. They could have soon begun to make plans to seize power in Israel, and if certain ancient prophecies had been correctly interpreted, then the messianic Kingdom would before long be spread to all nations. Judas would be there at the side of Jesus to help bring about all of these glorious victories. How heartbroken he was when Jesus threw away all of this popularity and potential glory with that strange and incomprehensible sermon about eating his flesh and drinking his blood (Jn 6:54). At the end of that sermon Judas was angry and felt the overwhelming desire to walk away from Jesus in protest, alongside the Galilean crowds, but somehow he forced himself to stay. It was then that Jesus warned that one of the Twelve was becoming like a devil (Jn 6:71).

Now, a year had passed, and since then Judas had experienced one shattered dream after another. He could see that Jesus would never rise to power, for he had turned the authorities in Jerusalem against him by his saying and doing things he knew would scandalise them. Judas realised he was risking his life by following Jesus. On the verge of leaving he had begun to steal more and more from the common purse in order to set himself up for the future and to compensate for the losses of the past three years, during which time he had been unable to work. In Bethany came the moment that pushed him not only to leave Christ but to betray him for money. He knew how to calculate for the future and to take care of himself, and it was this self-love that was the root of his downfall.

John presents Magdalene and Judas as two polar opposites. The first one loves Christ more than her own life; the second loves himself more than Christ or anything else in the world. One would give all she owns to help Jesus; the other goes so far as to steal from him. One is perfect generosity; one is greedy selfishness. One loves Christ and shows it publicly, not caring what anybody may think of her gestures; the other is always thinking about the opinion of others and working out how best to protect himself from all harm.

Mary's anointing of Jesus was probably not the first time her behaviour irritated Judas. From the beginning he probably thought it would be better for the image of the group if this notorious woman did not travel with them. Of course people thought poorly of them because of her. Back in Galilee there had been that embarrassing incident in the house of the Pharisee. At that time Judas had thought the same thing as the Pharisee, that her expressions of love for Christ were inappropriate. In Bethany, however, her actions were not only inappropriate but wasteful, and Judas could not keep silent about her foolishness.

A cry of indignation escaped from his lips, and his protest insinuated itself into the hearts of others who were present (Mt 26:8). It was a moment of eternal importance. The least that Judas expected Jesus to do was to agree that it might have been more useful to sell the perfume and feed the poor, who always seemed to be so dear to his heart; but to his astonishment, Jesus again defended the unworthy woman's actions just as he defended her from the judgement of the Pharisee and from Martha's perfectly reasonable complaint. Not only did Jesus defend her, but he told Judas to "let her alone" (Jn 12:7) to stop making trouble for her. At that moment, the apostolic journey of Judas came to end. His wounded pride could not tolerate Jesus' choice of the kind of follower he wanted. He could have had Judas on his side, a prudent and capable man, who would have helped him become the most influential person in the history of Israel, but instead he freely chose this wretched woman over him. The rest of the meal he spent in an awkward silence before finally slipping away from the group, seething with wrath.

The next time Judas appears in the Synoptics, he is before the high priest, asking him what price he is willing to pay for the life of Jesus (Mt 26:14–15). He haggled as though in a marketplace and managed to seal a deal for the miserable price that would be paid for the life of a slave (Ex 21:32). From the temple treasury a purse of coins used for purchasing animals for sacrifice was prepared for the High Priest, who procured from Judas the Lamb for the last valid sacrifice in Israel. Jesus was most likely killed on Friday, April 7, in the year 30, which would have been the fourteenth day of the month of Nisan, the day on which the Paschal lambs were slaughtered in Jerusalem.[4] The victims had to be procured on the tenth day of Nisan (Ex 12:3), which would have been the Monday of Holy Week. In the mysterious chain of events that led up to the Passion it would not be surprising if Holy Monday was the day on which Judas began negotiations for his thirty pieces of silver. It is shocking to think that the life of God was sold so cheaply and that Judas preferred a pocket full of coins to the friendship of Christ. Yet even today, how easily people betray and separate themselves from the Lord. They lose the joy of having his divine life within their souls, as well as an eternity of unimaginable happiness, for the pitiable pleasure of a moment.

Reclined at table in Bethany, on the night before he entered the City of the King, Jesus knew exactly how Judas had been feeling towards him and exactly what he was about to do. The bitterness of this betrayal was breaking his heart, but he would not expose the traitor in front of everybody. He would offer warnings and give him every chance to change and be saved, but alas one who falls from such a height is often the hardest to bring back. One of Christ's greatest sufferings began to pierce his heart: the knowledge that there will be souls who will reject his grace to the end and even die in their hatred of his divine will. The mystery of iniquity at work in

---

[4] Andres Fernandez, S.J., *The Life of Christ* (Westminster, Md.: Newman Press, 1958), p. 68.

the heart of Judas personifies all that is most repulsive in human nature, which Jesus was ready to die for. But as he looked upon the sincerity of Mary Magdalene's loving adoration, he could forget for a moment that he was in the presence of a treacherous thief. The resolution to persevere, to allow his own blood to be spilled for the salvation of souls like her, overpowered the bitterness of knowing that there were souls for whom his blood would be spilled in vain. When the time came for the final battle, as he went forward towards his agony in Gethsemane, the beautiful fragrance of spikenard still lingered in the air, to remind him of all that is worth redeeming in broken human nature. In order to bring that broken beauty back to its eternal perfection, he was ready to give his life.

The "memorial" of extravagant love

Mary's anointing of Christ teaches us how worthy Jesus is of the greatest sacrifices and the greatest expressions of our love. It is only because Magdalene's loving gesture is so extravagant that we are still talking about it today, as Jesus said we would (Mk 14:9). He was certainly anointed many times but none were as worthy of remembrance as this one. Lukewarmness is forgotten very quickly but ardent devotion never. Her example spurs us on to love Christ, not in a mediocre or ordinary manner but in the most extraordinary way possible, with concrete signs and expressions of how much he means to us. She could have sold this perfume and used the small fortune for many other things, but love made her lavish it all on Jesus. Love is loved in Bethany! Christ deserves only the best, but very often we lack generosity towards him. Instead of giving him what is most precious, especially our valuable time, sacrificed so as to be with him in prayer, we very often give him only what little time is left over, after we have first done all the other things we enjoy. We spend all of our time labouring for what will perish and not for that which endures forever (Jn 6:27).

Even in the heart of the Church we are very often lacking in generosity towards the Real Presence of Christ in the Eucharist. The sacred body that Mary anointed remains within us until the end of time in the Blessed Sacrament, but how often we find abandoned churches where nobody takes the time to pray before the tabernacle any more! Sometimes priests even discourage their parishioners from organising eucharistic adoration. When they see people wanting to spend time with Jesus, they cry out with Judas: "Why this waste?" Instead of asking them to offer their time in homage to Christ's divine majesty, some priests would rather persuade the faithful to spend all of their free time by participating in projects and meetings. How much time has been wasted on useless activities that have done nothing to bring more souls to Christ, while the source of grace, Christ himself, is not even consulted in prayer about his will for his Church? Jesus deserves a banquet of our time and love, but often we give him nothing but the leftovers. Time given to the eucharistic Lord or to the careful, reverent celebration of the liturgy is never time wasted but always contributes to the salvation of the world and the authentic renewal of the Church.

Something beautiful for Christ

In addition to giving Christ our time we should also en-
sure that everything related to the Eucharist is truly beautiful. Some say that Jesus does not want Church resources
spent on buildings and liturgies, but they seem to forget
that in this way they share the logic of Judas, which was
rebuked by the Lord himself. Divine worship requires
and deserves the very best of what we can offer. Jesus has
abased himself to remain with us in the Eucharist until the
end of time, and we should do all we can to exalt him in
every way possible. Sometimes people who frown upon
spending money to make eucharistic worship beautiful
live in great comfort themselves. They are happy to live
in mansions while the tabernacle remains in a state unworthy of the divine presence. We can only imagine what
Magdalene would say if she were here today to see the
ugliness and barrenness of some of our modern chapels
and tabernacles. Some parishes are even too stingy to surround the presence of the Lord with flowers and candles,
which have traditionally symbolized our faith and love.

Those who think they have no time and money for
the upkeep of the house of God would do well to take a
lesson from Saint Jean Vianney. The French parish priest
ate nothing but a couple of boiled potatoes every day and
wore worn-out clothes, but he spared no expense when it
came to the Blessed Sacrament. He walked to Lyon with
all of the money of the parish and was scarcely able to
find a monstrance magnificent enough for the worship
of the eucharistic Lord. In the Old Covenant the Jewish people would each contribute a half-shekel annually

in order to beautify the tabernacle, and it was promised that this contribution would "bring the sons of Israel to remembrance before the LORD" (Ex 30:16). Those who contribute to make eucharistic worship beautiful today will surely be remembered for their generous display of faith in the Real Presence of Christ. Down through the ages God's faithful people have been delighted to be able to offer sacrifices to show their faith and love for Jesus in the Blessed Sacrament. Nothing that we give to the Lord is ever wasted, for he rewards every sacrifice with a hundredfold generosity.

Today there are many debates about the beautiful gift of priestly celibacy, and the world is trying to convince the Church that such a sacrifice for love of Jesus is a waste. It is argued that we get only one life and that we should not throw it away by giving up marriage. Whenever a talented young person who could perhaps do something great in the world wants to renounce natural marriage for the higher good of spiritual marriage with God, people can be heard to say: "What a waste!" Such statements are understandable when they come from people with no faith, but this way of thinking should never find its way into the Church. Priestly celibacy is a powerful gift that the holy Catholic Church knows she must treasure. We should be delighted to see lives laid down for love of Jesus. The more beautiful that which is offered in homage to him the better. Similarly, there should be nothing more pleasing to the Church than seeing a young woman who loves Christ above all things and who is ready to enter into the cloistered state to live for love of him alone. It is like plucking up a rose to place it beside the tabernacle.

In one way the rose has ceased to live and will soon fade away, but it has been chosen to serve the noblest of all purposes. Blessed is the rose uprooted from the world with all of its vanities to become a bride of Christ. This is the kind of radical self-sacrificial love that the example of Mary Magdalene and the praise of Christ himself are still calling us to today.

To lead by the example of love

"She has done what she could" (Mk 14:8). This is the judgement of Christ upon the actions of Mary Magdalene. How lovely it would be if the just Judge were to one day say the same of us too. Jesus does not expect what is unreasonable, but at the end of our lives we should be able to say that we did the best we could, that we were perhaps weak but certainly loved Jesus faithfully. Then we can hope to hear those consoling words that Christ once addressed to his faithful in the Book of Revelation: "I know your works. Behold, I have set before you an open door, which no one is able to shut; I know that you have but little power, and yet you have kept my word and have not denied my name" (Rev 3:8).

Saint Faustina came to the realization that it is not the apparent greatness of our works that really counts but rather the love with which we carry them out. She wrote in her diary:

I have come to understand today that even if I did not accomplish any of the things the Lord is demanding of me, I know that I shall be rewarded as if I had fulfilled everything, because He sees the intention with which I begin, and even if He called me to Himself today, the work would not suffer at all by that, because He Himself is the Lord of both the work and the worker. My part is to love Him to folly; all works are nothing more than a tiny drop before Him. It is love that has meaning and power and merit. He has opened up great horizons in my soul—love compensates for the chasms.[5]

Sanctity consists primarily in loving Jesus faithfully, or as Saint Faustina put it, in loving him to folly! Some souls, such as Blessed Charles de Foucauld, did not accomplish extraordinary works in the Church during their lifetimes. They simply burned with the fire of love for Jesus Christ, and that was sufficient for them to be beatified. How few people really love Christ with a self-forgetful kind of love. How rare and how precious is a soul like Magdalene, faithful, simple and sincere! A soul like that is worth more to the life and mission of the Church than a thousand others. Even Jesus himself tells us that wherever in the whole world this Good News is preached, this woman's love for him should be told as an essential part of the story! She is the biblical prototype of pious souls, those who express their devotion by concrete acts of love. Such souls are often looked down upon by the supposedly more sophisticated, but the more we meditate upon Saint Magdalene, the more we learn to be cautious in judging people who publicly display their love for Jesus.

The word "piety" often carries a negative connotation, but we should not forget that piety is a gift of the Holy

[5] Saint Faustina, *Diary*, no. 822.

Spirit. It is true that pharisaical attention-seeking displays of piety are never praiseworthy, but when sincere love spills over into concrete expressions of devotion, such acts are very meritorious. Only Jesus, who sees the heart, can judge with justice, and so we should refrain from all judgement of souls and from harsh discouragement of pious devotions. When tempted to severity towards pious souls, we should recall Christ's words in defence of Magdalene: "Let her alone, she has done a beautiful thing to me."

In her anointing of Christ, Mary teaches all those who see her what kind of love and adoration the presence of Jesus deserves. The beautiful fragrance which symbolises her love and which fills the whole house is something those present would never be able to forget. In our days, when so many in the Church have forgotten how to love Christ and when his living presence in the Blessed Sacrament is so mistreated and ignored, adorers need to fill the entire house of the Church with the fragrance of their love. We need "Magdalenes of the Eucharist" whose example of "wasting" their time and energy in prolonged adoration will teach others that Christ is really present and that he deserves the perpetual presence of his Church before him.

Faith in the eucharistic Presence of Christ is often transmitted or destroyed by the physical gestures of others. Many stories are told which confirm this. A modern-day apostle of the Eucharist, whose humility would not allow him to be named, once shared the story of how he first came to believe in the Blessed Sacrament. He was a very young altar boy chosen to carry a candle for a eucharistic procession. He had been told about the Real Presence but refused to believe it was true. During the procession a man who saw Christ coming jumped out of his car and prostrated himself on the street before the monstrance. The young boy looked at the man and then looked back at the monstrance and received the gift of unshakeable faith in the Eucharist. This faith transformed his life. It was the result of a gesture that may have seemed radical to passers-by but was a powerful channel for divine grace. Faith is transmitted by hearing and by seeing! A similar thing happened to Archbishop Fulton Sheen, who was influenced in his decision never to miss daily adoration by the story of a young Chinese girl's display of love for the Blessed Sacrament. If only our parish celebrations of the Eucharist would do more to transmit visually the fire of eucharistic faith and love.

It is not just the example of adorers, however, that moves others; it is also the unseen graces being won by their faithful love for Jesus. The Lord does more than we can even hope for or imagine if we make sacrifices out of love for him. I was once called upon to start perpetual eucharistic adoration in the cathedral parish of an important French city. In France the crisis in faith was so bad that for decades adoration had completely disappeared in many places. The pastor of this particular parish, however, believed that perpetual eucharistic adoration simply had to begin in his parish. He would accept nothing less than an uninterrupted chain of love before the Blessed Sacrament and was prepared to do anything to bring it about. Shortly before I arrived, there had been a funeral in the parish of a true modern saint. Throughout the turbulent period of the second half of the twentieth century, this one faithful soul had continued to love and adore the Blessed Sacrament. He had somehow managed to obtain a key for the church from his pastor, and on his own he would go to the church every Thursday evening and spend the entire night prostrate before the tabernacle. In winter, the church was bitterly cold; but the fire of love in this man's soul was too strong to be hindered by such an obstacle, and for decades he kept the grace of eucharistic adoration alive in this region. The entrance of this man into the face-to-face adoration of the heavenly Jerusalem surely caused a generous rain of graces to descend upon the entire parish; there had to be a link between his fidelity and the mission to establish perpetual eucharistic adoration. Great victories in the Church are always obtained in the hiddenness of some faithful heart before they become visible. Perhaps the Lord deliberately chooses to hide the fruits of a person's faithful prayer until his arrival in the courts of heaven, where an unimaginable celebration of his accomplishments awaits him.

~

6

The First Consoler of
Jesus and Mary

Love triumphs in the midst of hatred, and the light shines
brighter when it is surrounded by darkness. We have seen
how Magdalene's love grew and grew, so that as the outrage of Judas' betrayal was about to be perpetrated, there
was a heart present to console the Sacred Heart. As the
enemies of Jesus organised the final phase of their cruel
plan, his heart of purest love was entering the final phase of
its own plan for the life of the world. As the soldiers with
the help of Judas were getting ready to make their way to
Gethsemane, in an ecstasy of love Christ bequeathed to
the world his last will and testament: the ineffable mystery
of the Eucharist. The most evil crime in human history
was thus interiorly transformed by Jesus into the greatest
act of self-giving love. He anticipated the Cross and the
spilling of his blood with a New Covenant consecration
that is the strength and the happiness of the Church until
the end of time. The divine blood was offered in advance
as a transforming gift, before wicked men had a chance to
spill it. Hatred had been outwitted and undone by Love.
Thanks to the anticipatory offering of the Eucharist, the
greatest crime in human history became the saving sacrifice that sanctifies the world.

Could you not watch?

With the inheritance of the precious eucharistic Blood bequeathed to the Church, the Passion began. Soldiers apprehended their Victim, and the merciful Holy Face, which had become the only joy of Mary Magdalene's heart, was disfigured beyond recognition. However, while still at table and before the light of the evening was engulfed by the darkness of Gethsemane, the thought of Jesus was not for himself but rather to console the hearts of his brothers. "Let not your hearts be troubled" (Jn 14:1). As a good father who must soon leave his children to depart for war gently prepares their little hearts for separation with words of love, so it was with Jesus before the warfare of the Passion. As soon as the luminous mystery of the Last Supper was celebrated and while the eucharistic species still remained in the hearts of the peace-filled apostles, with the traitor finally gone from their company, Jesus began to reveal to his apostles the deepest and most intimate truths about his love (Jn 13–14). It is as though the gift of the first Holy Communion opened up new levels of depth to the revelation of his infinite love, as well as to the love he expects from his friends.

During the long-awaited evening, after the Eucharist had been given, Jesus did not repeat what he said earlier to the crowds, "Love your neighbour as yourself." Rather, he gave the far more sublime command: "Love one another as I have loved you" (Jn 15:12). His words grow warmer and warmer as the moment of his exodus approaches. With this first eucharistic thanksgiving completed, Jesus instructed his new priests to arise from

table, for they must be on their way. With no further explanation about where they were going, Jesus walked out
into the night with his friends and continued to speak of
the mystery of what had just taken place in Holy Communion. The spellbound apostles knew that this was one
of those moments when they should not ask too many
questions but simply listen and ponder. Only later would
the Spirit of Truth unveil the meaning of the treasure that
their memories stored up. "I am the vine, you are the
branches", Jesus solemnly declared as they passed some
small vineyard on their way towards the Kidron Valley
(Jn 15:5). Even while the apostles' lips were still purpled
by the divine sap of his eucharistic Blood, Jesus explained
how he could love through their hearts so that they would
truly be able to love as he loved them and one day bear
"much fruit" (Jn 15:5). However, the happy memory of
this outpouring of sacramental grace and divine love was
soon to be mingled with tears and regrets for the apostles.

As they arrived in the garden to which Jesus had often
led them before, for evening prayer, something extremely
disturbing took place before Peter, James and John. The
other eight apostles had also noticed a change in Jesus as
they approached the Mount of Olives, as an anxious look
began to appear on his usually serene and kindly countenance. But Jesus had left them behind near the entrance
to the garden, for they would not have been able to bear
the sight of what was about to happen. Only the chosen
three, in whose memories the light of Tabor still lingered,
were allowed to accompany the Lord as the full extent
of the fragility he assumed on our behalf was manifested.
For the first time in three years the Master seemed to

break down and be crushed by a sadness, the cause of which he did not say. All he asked them to do was to stay awake and pray, which the three apostles were willing to do. As the hours passed and Jesus grew ever more anguished, a dark foreboding seized their souls too, and it was only sleep that allowed them some escape. As Jesus continued to pray even more earnestly in silence, he was tormented by visions so painful, that the sweat streaming from his forehead turned crimson (Lk 22:44). The sleep of the apostles was a restless one, filled with evil images and mocking thoughts about how their faith in Jesus had all been in vain, of how they had been led astray and cut themselves off from the holy people of Israel. It was the hour of scandal and the momentary reign of darkness (Mt 26:31; Lk 22:53).

Innocence meets guilt

So what was happening in the mind and soul of Jesus Christ that night? What anguish could be so great that it turns beads of sweat into streams of blood? It was the night on which the sinless one became sin for our sake (2 Cor 5:21). Before the justice of God, the innocent Lamb took my guilt and yours upon him as though it were his own. There in Gethsemane, the place where olives were once pressed to make oil, the soul of Jesus was crushed, so that we might one day receive the healing oil of mercy. He stood before the Father with the immense burden all of my sins upon his soul. It was a monstrous weight to bear for a Victim so pure, so holy, so spotless in every way. A conscience so immaculate should never come in contact with such shameful wickedness, but he had to behold it all, so that my conscience could be washed clean. In my name he had to make not only the perfect act of expiation but even the perfect act of contrition. He had to choose to undergo what it is almost impossible for a human will to choose, and in that choice, every evil choice since the first choice of Adam, was reversed. With one heroic act of will, one mighty *Fiat* he overturned the original sin and set in motion the reparation of every subsequent sin that has ever been chosen. In this most courageous of all acts in human history, the Son of God merited for us the grace to return to union with the divine will, something which had had been lost since Eden.

Blessed John Henry Newman describes the frightening moment when our sins invaded the innocent mind of Christ and when, seizing upon this moment, the enemy who had retreated in the desert found his "opportune time" (Lk 4:13) to pounce:

> There He knelt, motionless and still, while the vile and horrible fiend clad His spirit in a robe steeped in all that is hateful and heinous in human crime, which clung close round His heart, and filled His conscience, and found its way into every sense and pore of His mind, and spread over Him a moral leprosy, till He almost felt Himself to be that which He never could be, and which His foe would fain have made Him. Oh, the horror, when He looked, and did not know Himself, and felt as a foul and loathsome sinner, from His vivid perception of that mass of corruption which poured over His head and ran down even to the skirts of His garments! Oh, the distraction, when He found His eyes, and hands, and feet,

and lips, and heart, as if the members of the Evil One, and not of God! Are these the hands of the Immaculate Lamb of God, once innocent, but now red with ten thousand barbarous deeds of blood? are these His lips, not uttering prayer, and praise, and holy blessings, but as if defiled with oaths, and blasphemies, and doctrines of devils? or His eyes, profaned as they are by all the evil visions and idolatrous fascinations for which men have abandoned their adorable Creator? And His ears, they ring with sounds of revelry and of strife; and His heart is frozen with avarice, and cruelty, and unbelief; and His very memory is laden with every sin which has been committed since the fall. . . . Oh, who does not know the misery of a haunting thought which comes again and again, in spite of rejection, to annoy, if it cannot seduce? or of some odious and sickening imagination, in no sense one's own, but forced upon the mind from without? or of evil knowledge, gained with or without a man's fault, but which he would give a great price to be rid of at once and for ever? And adversaries such as these gather around Thee, Blessed Lord, in millions now; they come in troops more numerous than the locust or the palmerworm, or the plagues of hail, and flies, and frogs, which were sent against Pharaoh. Of the living and of the dead and of the as yet unborn, of the lost and of the saved, of Thy people and of strangers, of sinners and of saints, all sins are there. Thy dearest are there, Thy saints and Thy chosen are upon Thee; Thy three Apostles, Peter, James, and John; but not as comforters, but as accusers, like the friends of Job, sprinkling dust towards heaven (see Job 2:12), and heaping curses on Thy head. All are there but one; one only is not there, one only; for she who had no part in sin, she only could console Thee, and therefore she is not nigh. She will be near Thee on the Cross, she is separated from Thee in the garden. She has been Thy companion and Thy confidant through Thy life, she interchanged with Thee the pure thoughts and holy meditations of thirty years; but her virgin ear may not take in, nor may her immaculate heart conceive, what now is in vision before Thee. None was equal to the weight but God; sometimes before Thy saints Thou hast brought the image of a single sin, as it appears in the light of Thy countenance, or of venial sins, not mortal; and they have told us that the sight did all but kill them, nay, would have killed them, had it not been instantly withdrawn. The Mother of God, for all her sanctity, nay by reason of it, could not have borne even one brood of that innumerable progeny of Satan which now compasses Thee about. It is the long history of a world, and God alone can bear the load of it. Hopes blighted, vows broken, lights quenched, warnings scorned, opportunities lost; the innocent betrayed, the young hardened, the penitent relapsing, the just overcome, the aged failing; the sophistry of misbelief, the wilfulness of passion, the obduracy of pride, the tyranny of habit, the canker of remorse, the wasting fever of care, the anguish of shame, the pining of disappointment, the sickness of despair; such cruel, such pitiable spectacles, such heartrending, revolting, detestable, maddening scenes; nay, the haggard faces, the convulsed lips, the flushed cheek, the dark brow of the willing slaves of evil, they are all before Him now; they are upon Him and in Him. They are with Him instead of that ineffable peace which has inhabited His soul since the moment of His conception. They are upon Him, they are all but His own; He cries to His Father as if He were the criminal, not the Victim; His agony takes the form of guilt and compunction. He is doing penance, He is making confession, He is exercising contrition, with a reality and a virtue infinitely greater than that of all saints and penitents together; for He is the One Victim for us all, the sole Satisfaction, the real Penitent, all but the real sinner.[1]

As Christ's generous heart deigned to undergo such an unbearable ordeal for the sake of sinners, he had the right to expect that at least some sinners, the ones he had just called friends (Jn 15:15), would stay awake and be with him in his hour of agony. We all want company in a time of terrible sorrow. We want to be holding the hand of a loved one as the darkness of grief descends upon us. The mere presence of one who loves us lightens the burden of our pain, but on the one night that Jesus Christ truly needed his friends, their love was not strong enough to accompany him to the bitter end. "I looked for pity, but there was none; and for comforters, but I found none" (Ps 69:20).

Had Magdalene been there, she would have no doubt had enough fire in her loving passionate heart to remain awake. With deep feminine intuition of the heart, she would have sensed the gravity of this crisis and the response of love it demanded. One so attentive to every movement of the heart of Jesus would never have allowed his heart to break in such bitter solitude. However, it was not ordained that the physical presence of Mary Magdalene should be the consolation of Christ in Gethsemane. On that night she had begun to fulfil another part of her vocation of love, and it was to console the immaculate

[1] John Henry Newman, "The Mental Sufferings of Our Lord in His Passion", Sermon 16 of *Discourses Addressed to Mixed Congregations* (London: Longmans, Green, and Co., 1906), pp. 335–41.

heart of the Mother who could sense from afar what was happening in the heart of her only beloved Son. One Passion was beginning to take hold of two hearts that night, and by the same time the following evening both of those hearts would be pierced through, one physically, one spiritually (Lk 2:35). One heart would be lying lifeless in a cold tomb of stone, the other still beating but dead in a tomb of grief. The loving, faithful presence of Saint Mary Magdalene was a balm on the wounds of both of these broken innocent hearts. Again we see how precious and how rare in this world is a heart that simply understands how to love.

The kiss of death

The dreaded moment in which the treachery of an apostle was unveiled for all to see arrived, the moment that has become synonymous with all that is vile in human nature. Judas came to the entrance of Gethsemane, at the head of a huge crowd, armed for battle. Following a satanic inspiration he decided to betray Jesus by laying a stinging kiss upon his Holy Face. The thought of this gesture gave his hardened heart a perverse thrill of excitement. In front of the outraged and furious apostles, one of their own number emerged from the darkness of the olive groves and boldly approached the gentle Master. Not only did he hand him over to torture and death, but he dared to do so with a kiss! The meek and forgiving heart of Jesus did not react with the disgust and anger merited by such an abominable betrayal, but rather with a question: "Friend why are you here?" (Mt 26:50). Friend, why? Why would you do such a thing? Why would anybody betray One who has done nothing but show him love? What kind of diabolical logic is behind such an idea? What is this mystery of iniquity in your heart? Even the One who knows and understands all things seemed perplexed before the free choice to commit such a sin. What is at the root of the sin of betrayal? Pride, vanity, greed, jealousy? "Friend, why?" This divine question rings out across human history, from the days of Adam to those of the Antichrist.

The study of the biblical texts in the original language that the Holy Spirit inspired often brings out deeper layers of meaning. The word that describes the nature of the kiss of Judas is worthy of reflection. The Greek verb that means "to kiss" is one with the verb that means "to love" (*phileo*). It is a gesture that is designed by the Creator to express love. A mother naturally wants to kiss her baby. Through a kiss we speak with our bodies the language of love. A kiss should be the revelation of what is in the heart and intention of the person. Judas told a flagrant lie with the gesture of his body. The love that a kiss expresses was on his lips, but not in his heart.

How many people lie today with their bodies! The language of the body that human sexuality expresses has been so debased in the last half century that people no longer even understand what they are doing by their gestures. Since the advent of this contraceptive epoch in which we live, many men and women use an act that signifies irrevocable self-gift and openness to bringing new life into the world through love, solely to obtain egotistical pleasures of the flesh. It is a betrayal, not only of the

Creator, but also of self and of the other immortal creature being used like some kind of apparatus for pleasure.
The language of the human soul, a language expressed
by the body, but whose gestures have eternal repercus-
sions, has been smothered under the insatiable tyranny
of carnal passions. The destructive consequences of this
selfish mentality, condoned by our culture, have been too
many to enumerate. They include the innocent blood of
millions of unborn victims. But it is not only in the area
of human sexuality that we can lie with the body. How
many Catholics arise from bended knee and approach the
altar of Holy Communion with "amen" on their lips but
unbelief in their hearts?

There is another detail about the kiss of Judas that is
worthy of note. The word for "kiss" that the evangelist
employs is not the ordinary one. It is the word that de-
notes an emphatic kiss (*kataphileo*). It is the kind of kiss
that expresses the deepest sentiments of love. It was the
kind of kiss with which the long lost prodigal son was
welcomed home by his father (Lk 15:20). We all know
this kind of kiss; it is usually accompanied by tears of
love! The nature of this kiss made the treachery of Judas
all the more painful for Christ. In the sickness of his mind,
the traitor decided to feign intense love for Jesus, in the
very moment he was handing him over to be condemned
and murdered. Coincidentally, or perhaps providentially,
this very word, which only appears a handful of times in
the New Testament, is also the word used to describe the
holy kisses that penitent Magdalene once laid upon the
feet of Christ (Lk 7:45). Her kisses came straight from
the depth of her authentic loving heart. She who became

the antithesis of the traitor was unconsciously making reparation in advance to Christ, on behalf of all of mankind, for the bitter kiss of Judas. She may not have understood anything at the time, but the Holy Spirit who inspired her gestures, as well as the words that record them, knew that the memory of her tenderness would never be erased from the memory of the One who was not bound by the limits of time. For every Judas who breaks the heart of Christ, in all the treacherous kisses of human history, let us pray that there is a Magdalene.

He seemed no longer human

As the condemnation of Christ was finally pronounced by the corrupt high priest Caiaphas, there was a frightening moment in which the Lord's face is entirely covered over and struck by all who were standing nearby (Mt 26:67–68; Mk 14:65; Lk 22:63–65). The Greek verbs make clear that only after the face of Jesus is veiled do they begin to strike it with their fists. He had been slapped by one sycophant of the high priest beforehand, but it was only after his face was veiled that he began to be viciously punched by those present. It was almost as though his face was too innocent and holy to disfigure until it had been veiled. Some crimes, such as the murder of unborn children, could never be committed if we could only see the face of the victim. The human face is a mysterious thing. In the Greek language used by the evangelists, the word for "face" can also mean "person" or "presence". The mystery of the face reveals the identity of the person and to strike the face of another is to display fierce hatred for his person and even a desire to rid the world of his presence. This was the diabolical fury that was unleashed upon Christ in the early hours of the Passion. By the time Magdalene would see him in the Praetorium the following morning, his face which had always shown her nothing but tender kindness would be beaten, bruised and bathed in precious blood. After the Roman soldiers added their own brutal strength to the torture of the Saviour, and when he finally arrived on the hill of Calvary the prophesy of Isaiah would be realised: "His appearance was so marred, beyond human semblance" (Is 52:14). The shock that would grip her heart in the moment she first saw him on Good Friday would almost have been enough to take her very life itself. That divine gaze, those holy eyes which had transformed Mary's sinful heart back in Galilee were now dimmed with grief and could scarcely be opened for blood. How could such perfect innocence be condemned and suffer like a sinner? Never could she even imagine such a sight. How could the Master, who was always so calmly in control of everything, the Rock upon which her faith was built, now be so sorely humiliated? How could such majesty be annihilated and now be on the verge of total destruction? Some of the disciples were suggesting that he had somehow lost his holy power, while his enemies were triumphantly boasting that he was rejected by God. Magdalene knew that neither of these two blasphemous assertions was possible. In spite of her shock there was only one thing that she was sure of: that her love for Jesus was now even greater than ever before. The splendour of his adorable divine person did not seem to be diminished by the destruction of his outward appearance, but if anything it seemed to be enhanced. It was almost as though this horrible nightmare was only serving to reveal to the heart of Magdalene new depths of love hidden in the heart of Jesus. Nothing quite moves the heart like beholding the silent lamb surrounded by fierce wolves. When the guilty suffer, the heart is often touched by compassion but when the innocent suffer a loving heart will go as far as to desire to take their place. All Mary could do was think of how grateful she was to have met Jesus and to regret that she had not spent even more time rejoicing in his presence. Very often we do not know how blessed we are by some privilege until it is about to be taken from us. She realised now that the only thing that really mattered to her in this world was Christ's Real Presence.

What is this mystery of divine power which makes itself weak and even undergoes humiliation out of love for us? It is a mystery that our proud minds cannot fully comprehend, but our hearts can perceive that Love is never more loveable than when it makes itself vulnerable. This mystery of the Passion is prolonged and made present by the Sacrament of the Eucharist, where the One who has the power to "scatter hoarfrost like ashes" (Ps 147:17) is present behind the fragile appearances of bread and wine. The Cross and the Blessed Sacrament are part of the one holy mystery of divine vulnerability, which melted the heart of Mary Magdalene two thousand years ago and which continues to bring tears to our eyes to this day.

In his magnificent hymn *Adoro Te Devote* the angelic intellect of Saint Thomas Aquinas could only admire with awe how on the Cross Jesus hid his divinity but how in the Eucharist he goes even further and hides his very humanity. Blessed is the one who can profess faith in both the divinity and the humanity that are veiled behind the fragility of a little white Host. They will receive blessings akin to the small group of faithful souls who remained firm in faith on Calvary. They were perhaps unable to understand what was happening before their eyes, yet they remained firm in their faith in Jesus nonetheless. We cannot fully comprehend the mystery of the Eucharist, but we still profess with Saint Jean Vianney: "He is there!" Are we as grateful for his Real Presence as Mary Magdalene was two thousand years ago? Or as Saint Jean Vianney was one hundred and fifty years ago? Do we weep tears of grateful love as he did when he looked at the tabernacle?

The gaze of love

Magdalene would have done anything to be able to take away the pain of Christ Crucified but she knew that all she was able to do for him was to be present, to look and to love. During the hours of the Passion she knew that her place was beside the sorrowful Mother of Jesus to comfort and console her immaculate heart and with her to try and somehow console the heart of Christ. As the Lord was being scourged and mocked before all of Jerusalem, as he was being ridiculed, while he stood in a puddle of his own blood before Pilate, Magdalene feared that the Mother of Jesus would die of sorrow while she held her trembling hand; but somehow her broken maternal heart found the strength to follow the bloody footprints of her Son as he traced the first Way of the Cross over the rough stones of Jerusalem. Along that *Via Dolorosa*, the blood of Christ was mingled with the tears of his Mother, as well as the tears of Magdalene, which flowed more abundantly now than ever before.

At some point along that dark journey to Calvary, it is possible that Mary Magdalene began to have some intuition that what Christ was going through was somehow connected to our sins, that the joy of mercy which she had received had only come to her because of the loving sacrifice of Jesus, who had chosen to lay down his life for us. She could not understand it fully but perhaps she somehow perceived that he had taken on himself the pain of her guilt so that she could now live in the joy of his innocence. The words of Christ himself had hinted at the necessity of his suffering (Mk 8:31; 10:32–34) and the Blessed Virgin had no doubt explained something of this mystery to her on Holy Thursday evening. She had heard that John the Baptist had once said something about Jesus taking the sins of the world upon himself like a sacrificial lamb and the memory of this unusual prophecy now came back to mind. From the very first day she had met Jesus, she had indeed had the impression that his presence had somehow taken her sins away from her. Maybe this thought caused a new sword of grief to pierce her soul followed by a new surge of grateful love for Christ. She could have guessed that he did this out of nothing but pure love for her, to set her free, and all she could feel in her soul was that she was enveloped by the love

coming from Christ's gentle heart, whose beat was growing weaker and weaker by the minute. "Greater love has
no man than this, that a man lay down his life for his
friends" (Jn 15:13). As she reached the height of Calvary
her love for Christ rose to new heights and all she could
think of was how she wanted to let him know that he
was still loved, as she watched him drowning in a sea of
hatred. For a long time now, grace had been preparing
her for this moment. Her love was now strong enough
to console both Jesus and his broken-hearted Mother in
their hour of need.

As the noise of the hammer-blows rang out on the
hilltop of Calvary and as the cold nails pierced through
his flesh and bones, she heard a most beautiful cry come
forth from his lips. It summed up what must have been the
prayer which constantly rose from his heart: "Father, forgive them; for they know not what they do" (Lk 23:34).
Magdalene knew that this was the way he always looked
upon poor sinners and for a long time now she could no
longer bring herself to doubt that even the gravest of sins
could find forgiveness in the heart of Jesus; but to hear
him say these words about the very men who were trying to make him suffer as much as possible and who were
literally torturing the very life out of his young healthy
body, was astounding even for Magdalene. These words
were the expression of a heart too beautiful for human
minds to understand. These were the words of pure divine love. The Gospel of John brings us to the final moments of the Passion where Magdalene is looking on as
death finally starts to take hold of the One she loved more
than her life itself:

When the soldiers had crucified Jesus they took his garments and made four parts, one for each soldier; also his tunic. But the tunic was without seam, woven from top to bottom; so they said to one another, "Let us not tear it, but cast lots for it to see whose it shall be." This was to fulfil the Scripture,

> "They parted my garments among them,
> and for my clothing they cast lots."

So the soldiers did this. But standing by the cross of Jesus were his mother, and his mother's sister, Mary the wife of Clopas, and Mary Magdalene. When Jesus saw his mother, and the disciple whom he loved standing near, he said to his mother, "Woman, behold, your son!" Then he said to the disciple, "Behold, your mother!" And from that hour the disciple took her to his own home.

After this Jesus, knowing that all was now finished, said (to fulfil the Scripture), "I thirst." A bowl full of vinegar stood there; so they put a sponge full of the vinegar on hyssop and held it to his mouth. When Jesus had received the vinegar, he said, "It is finished" and he bowed his head and gave up his spirit. (Jn 19:23–30)

Mary Magdalene's mission in life was to love Jesus Christ with all of the strength of her passionate heart. This was what she had been created for, to be there for Jesus in his hour of darkness. This was all she had to concentrate on doing and divine providence would take care of everything else for her. She began to learn how to live this vocation a long time before the Passion, back in peaceful Galilee. As she felt the overwhelming urge to go and adore the Lord for the first time, in the house of the Pharisee, little did she know that in following this inspiration she was being called into her sublime mission to make reparation to the Sacred Heart of Jesus. She had been called into the life of Christ to repair the sin of the Pharisee who had been too proud to pay the Master the respect he deserved. At several other moments along the way there were similar experiences in which she knew her love was a consolation to the wounded heart of the Saviour. Nowhere was this more true than in the supper at Bethany, where her love for Jesus which had grown more radical and more boldly extravagant along the way, was called upon to console the Lord as he was about to be betrayed by one of his own beloved friends. Now on Calvary her love for Christ had reached its seraphic highpoint, precisely so that she would be ready to console the Lord in the moment he needed her most. In its most important hour human history needed a Mary Magdalene to be there for Jesus and Mary. This poor broken sinner who had been transformed into an angelic adorer of the heart of Christ was not called to do anything on Calvary except love. When Saint John, who had abandoned Christ the night before, but who had somehow found his way back into the court of the high priest and now into the company of the Virgin Mary and Magdalene, describes for us the scene of Christ's death, he clearly seems to contrast the attitude of the two groups at the foot of the Cross. On one hand there is the attitude of the barbaric soldiers who by now are probably half-drunk and who have been using the body of Christ for a few hours of cruel Roman-style entertainment. While on the other hand there stands the consolers of the Sacred Heart. The attitudes of both groups could not be more different and that of the latter is making amends for that of the former.

"So the soldiers did this. But standing by the cross of Jesus were his mother, and his mother's sister, Mary the wife of Clopas, and Mary Magdalene" (Jn 19:25).

The soldiers had just torn the limbs of Christ asunder, to such a degree that his body was now fighting to take its final breaths. Then they noticed that one of his garments was well made (no doubt by his Mother) and felt that it would be a shame to tear it (Jn 19:24). They had felt no sense of regret in tearing open his innocent flesh but tearing apart a valuable garment they felt would be wasteful and wrong. They treat a dead material object with more respect than a living Divine Person. This is where Magdalene's vocation of loving reparation reaches its supreme moment. Along with the Blessed Virgin Mary she is present at the Cross in order to counterbalance this barbaric treatment of God Incarnate. She knows that his presence in this world is of infinite value. Every second he is with us is more precious than anything else in this universe. She is called upon to believe that at the foot of the Cross, to hold that truth in her heart and simply to look into the eyes of Christ. In other words she is called upon to look at Christ with the tender love of a deep contemplative heart and in that act she has fulfilled the goal of her existence.

The outrage of this scene rightly provokes strong emotions from our hearts but the objective truth of that situation is not confined to the bitter history of Calvary. Jesus Christ is alive and present, body, blood, soul and divinity in the tabernacle of every one of our churches. The same Jesus who hung upon the Cross and who received the love of Magdalene is now waiting to be loved in the Blessed

Sacrament. We Catholics must examine our consciences and see if our treatment of Christ in the Eucharist resembles that of Magdalene or that of other characters in the Passion? Is Jesus Christ not treated like a dead object today? He once said as much to Saint Faustina. He said to her that when he comes in Holy Communion we treat him like a dead object, or a dead "thing" as it can also be translated.[2] When we enter our churches do we go to the tabernacle to visit our Saviour? Do we gaze upon him with love as did Mary Magdalene, or do we ignore him as though he were a dead object? Do we priests handle his sacred eucharistic flesh with tender care or do we manhandle and mistreat him as did Roman soldiers? Do we allow him to be handed over to those who should never be allowed to touch him, as the high priest once handed his Messiah over to the pagan powers of Rome? The effects of careless treatment of his body in its eucharistic state may not be the same as the manhandling of his mortal flesh, but the outrage is similar. The body is present under a different mode of being but the Divine Person present there is identical. What has happened to the beautiful reverence we once had for that sacred eucharistic Presence? There seems to be a form of spiritual insanity that has entered into the way many treat the Blessed Sacrament today, or is it simply a blatant lack of faith? At the end of our lives we will see how foolish we were to neglect such a treasure. We may not be able to make the entire Church

[2] Faustina Kowalska, *The Diary: Divine Mercy in My Soul* (Stockbridge, Mass.: Marian Press, 2003), no. 1385.

come back to awe and reverence for the Blessed Sacrament, but we can repair the evil by spending long periods of time in loving eucharistic adoration. Mary Magdalene knew she could not prevent the soldiers from mistreating Jesus but she could love him and this love nobody could take from her. What the Church needs today above all, if we are to make up for the unceasing torrent of sacrileges and outrages that flood the sanctuary, are souls who know how to gaze like Magdalene into the eyes of the eucharistic Jesus.

~

7

Apostle to the Apostles

After the horrors of Calvary and the painful experience of unfastening Christ's body from the Cross, then hurriedly trying to conclude its burial before the beginning of the Sabbath, Mary Magdalene and the other holy women were left feeling physically numb. Sleep was impossible, prayer was impossible, coherent conversation was impossible. All Mary had left were her tears. Her mind was filled with images of the Passion and at almost every moment she could still hear the agonising groans of Christ as he was nailed to the Cross, or the terrible sound of the death rattle as he gasped for his last breaths. It was as though he had been drowning before her eyes and she had not been able to reach out a hand to help him. Upon her memory she had engraved the last few seconds in which he still had life within him and how she longed to go back and stop that life from leaving this world. She would give anything to hear one word from his sacred lips or to catch one glimpse of his holy eyes. His blessed countenance had always been like a cold draught of water to her parched soul, but now that face was gone forever. Even the pain of her brother's death was nothing compared to this grief. At least Lazarus had died with dignity and surrounded by love, but Jesus had died while the chief priests were still mocking and laughing at him. It was as though they had been vindicated and Christ put to shame. She could no longer think straight about anything and had no more desire to live. The world was now a dark and miserable den of cruel sinners. Its light was gone. As she played the scenes of Calvary over again and again in her mind there was only one thought which would well up in her heart and bring her a moment's consolation: as soon as she could she would run to that tomb, find somebody to roll back the stone and redo the funeral anointing that she felt ashamed to have had to conclude so abruptly. That way she would try to get one last glimpse of his holy face and one last chance to cling to his sacred feet. With this resolution she found at least some moments of distraction from the pain. She began to round up the other holy women to help her find the most precious perfumes and spices available for the anointing. However she did not want to disturb the Mother of Jesus who since Friday afternoon had scarcely uttered a word. The Mother of Jesus was to be left alone and the good Apostle John would see to it that she was taken care of.

Such must have been the scene as Holy Saturday gave way to Easter Sunday. The next time we see her in sacred Scripture, Saint Mary Magdalene will be running through the streets of Jerusalem towards the hill of Calvary. So eager was her desire to be in the presence of Christ's dead body once again that she broke away from the group of holy women and arrived on her own before even the rising sun had shed its light upon her. The glorious account of the apparition of the risen Christ to Saint Mary

Magdalene is not in need of any embellishment with our clumsy human words. The scene is so marvellously described by Saint John that we will present it in its entirety without breaking it up for explanation. It is best to ponder very slowly over these inspired words of sacred Scripture before attempting to comment upon them. To each person this text speaks in a personal and unique manner.

> Now on the first day of the week, Mary Magdalene came to the tomb early, while it was still dark, and saw that the stone had been taken away from the tomb. So she ran, and went to Simon Peter and the other disciple, the one whom Jesus loved, and said to them, "They have taken the Lord out of the tomb, and we do not know where they have laid him." Peter then came out with the other disciple, and they went toward the tomb. They both ran, but the other disciple outran Peter and reached the tomb first; and stooping to look in, he saw the linen cloths lying there, but he did not go in. Then Simon Peter came, following him, and went into the tomb; he saw the linen cloths lying, and the napkin, which had been on his head, not lying with the linen cloths but rolled up in a place by itself. Then the other disciple, who reached the tomb first, also went in, and he saw and believed; for as yet they did not know the Scripture, that he must rise from the dead. Then the disciples went back to their homes.
>
> But Mary stood weeping outside the tomb, and as she wept she stooped to look into the tomb; and she saw two angels in white, sitting where the body of Jesus had lain, one at the head and one at the feet. They said to her, "Woman, why are you weeping?" She said to them, "Because they have taken away my Lord, and I do not know where they have laid him." Saying this, she turned

round and saw Jesus standing, but she did not know that it was Jesus. Jesus said to her, "Woman, why are you weeping? Whom do you seek?" Supposing him to be the gardener, she said to him, "Sir, if you have carried him away, tell me where you have laid him, and I will take him away." Jesus said to her, "Mary." She turned and said to him in Hebrew, "Rabboni!" (which means Teacher). Jesus said to her, "Do not hold me, for I have not yet ascended to the Father; but go to my brethren and say to them, I am ascending to my Father and your Father, to my God and your God." Mary Magdalene went and said to the disciples, "I have seen the Lord"; and she told them that he had said these things to her. (Jn 20:1–18)

Why Magdalene?

As mentioned above, several women set out to anoint Christ's body on Easter Sunday, but Mary Magdalene seems to have arrived before all the others; and according to Saint John she was the first to see the risen Christ. There is a very ancient tradition that says that while Jesus was away from the tomb, before Magdalene saw him, he was privately appearing to his Most Blessed Mother, the only one who truly knew he would rise, and so who had no need to go to the empty tomb in order to anoint his body. In a faith like that of the Virgin Mary, there were no doubts or confused misinterpretations of what Christ meant when he clearly said he would rise from the dead (Mt 16:21). She who was called "blessed" because she always believed in God's Word (Lk 1:45) would have clung to the truth of Christ's Resurrection prophecy with all the strength of her immaculate will. It was perhaps what

kept her from dying of grief on Good Friday. In his cate-
chesis for May 21, 1997, Saint John Paul II revealed his
own belief in the truth of this tradition. Here is how the
Holy Father explained it:

> Indeed, it is legitimate to think that the Mother was prob-
> ably the first person to whom the risen Jesus appeared.
> Could not Mary's absence from the group of women who
> went to the tomb at dawn (cf. Mk 16:1; Mt 28:1) indicate
> that she had already met Jesus? This inference would also
> be confirmed by the fact that the first witnesses of the
> Resurrection, by Jesus' will, were the women who had
> remained faithful at the foot of the Cross and therefore
> were more steadfast in faith. Indeed, the Risen One en-
> trusts to one of them, Mary Magdalene, the message to
> be passed on to the Apostles (cf. Jn 20:17–18). Perhaps
> this fact too allows us to think that Jesus showed himself
> first to his Mother, who had been the most faithful and
> had kept her faith intact when put to the test.[1]

Mary Magdalene was nonetheless chosen to receive an
apparition of the Risen Lord well before all of the other
disciples. Saint Thomas Aquinas says the reason why Jesus
appears to Mary Magdalene before he appears to the others is that she was more ardent and devoted to Christ
than his other followers. He goes back to the statement
of Jesus in the early days of her conversion to find a clue.
Jesus publicly praised her from the very beginning and
said that her many sins had been erased because she loved
so much.[2] Aquinas shows how it is above all her intense
love that draws down upon her the predilection of the

---

[1] Pope John Paul II, General Audience, May 21, 1997.
[2] Thomas Aquinas, *Commentary on the Gospel of John*, 2472, 2493.

Lord. Wisdom hastens to reveal itself to those who desire it above all other things (Wis 6:14). Some readers are surprised that in his commentary on the Gospel of John, it seems so natural for Saint Thomas to make the connection between the sinful woman who anoints Christ in Galilee, Mary of Bethany and Mary Magdalene; but we must remember that he was writing long before any of this was being called into question in the Roman Catholic Church.

Mary's love obtained for her this blessing from the Lord, and in giving her this privilege it would also seem that Christ was teaching us a lesson about his mercy and the fact that sinners can hope to be counted among his most blessed friends. Jesus chose Magdalene to be present at the foot of the Cross and to be the first to the empty tomb so as to show us how his Paschal Mystery was destined to transform the greatest sinners into the greatest saints. With the Resurrection of Jesus the mystery of salvation was accomplished, and it is Saint Mary Magdalene who received the first fruits of redemption and the joy it brings to the human heart. She saw two angels, one where the head of Christ lay, the other where his feet once were. Is the earthly angel of adoration perhaps being reminded by these two heavenly angels of the consolation she brought to Christ by her anointings of his head and feet? The love of this faithful soul has merited the joy of Easter here below and a high place in heaven hereafter.

Weeping like a Magdalene

So synonymous is Mary Magdalene with tears that the French have a popular expression: "*pleurer comme une Madeleine*", that is to say, "to weep like a Magdalene". A heart that loves much weeps often and since she first stepped onto the stage of Scripture this marvellous creature has shed a veritable river of tears. Magdalene was crying because the body of Jesus is gone. She would have been inconsolable at the empty tomb because the closest thing to the Real Presence of Christ was now absent. Perhaps she had hoped to be able to pray at the tomb and ponder the holy bones of the One who had brought her such joy. Peter and John had gone to their homes but Magdalene would not leave. For how long would she have remained weeping at the empty tomb? She seemed to be intent on going nowhere and were he not already risen those holy tears would nearly have been enough to bring him back from the dead. The Lord rushes to calm the pain of his friends and he is always close to the broken hearted, those whose spirit is crushed. Only those who have rejected him are left in despair. They have chosen freely to distance themselves from him and so out of respect for their freedom he does not draw near. Often our tears have something of self-pity and self-love, but these tears of Magdalene were the purest of tears, tears for Christ, welling up from a heart that loved him alone. Worthy of divine consolation were such tears. Then a mysterious voice from behind her said: "Why are you weeping?" (Jn 20:15). This question was designed to make her think of the reason for her tears which made her loving longing for Jesus burn even more ardently.

A question often draws out the formulation of a desire. When we speak about our desires they get stronger than when they just exist within us. This was her desire: she absolutely had to be in the presence of Christ as soon as possible, if not she would lose her mind or die of sorrow. Jesus was her only thought. Jesus brought the fire of her desire to its highest blaze and then fulfils it in a way more marvellous than what she had actually been desiring. For his beloved friends he does more than we can even hope for. The way we understand our divinely inspired desires is often too human to anticipate the divine generosity.

Magdalene's desire was for Jesus, but she only thought of being in the presence of his dead body. However he desired to go further and put her in the presence of his living body. It is true that he told her not to cling to him just yet and she would soon have to depart from the Real Presence of that sacred body, but later she would be allowed to cling to him in a far more extraordinary way. It was a beautiful thing to behold the living body of Jesus standing before her, but it is a far more beautiful thing to be able to receive that sacred body into her heart in the Eucharist and then to cling to him for all eternity in heaven. Earlier we mentioned that the story of Mary's life was one of unfulfilled desire leading to greater fulfilment. This upward spiral of ever greater happiness continues through the mystery of the Resurrection, then in the gift of the Eucharist and finally up into the ecstasy of eternity. It is the same for all of us. This present joy we have found in encountering Christ and even discovering his Real Presence in the Eucharist is only the beginning of our fulfilment. We are still in the shadows of the valley of death and even here the divine generosity is astounding. We cannot even begin to imagine what the joys of heaven will be like!

"Whom do you seek?"

"Whom do you seek?" There is more to this question than might initially meet the eye. It was not the first time Jesus had addressed this kind of question to his disciples. He is always questioning the heart or we might say the intention of the person. The first question he addressed to his apostles was: "What do you seek?" (Jn 1:38). What was Mary really seeking in seeking Jesus? What was she seeking when she first came to him almost three years earlier? Nobody can say for certain, but it was most likely forgiveness for her sins and a chance to start her life all over again. This was the deep driving motive of her drawing near to Jesus Christ and this she found. What was she seeking now that her sins were long forgiven? Had her desire for forgiveness really become pure love for Christ? Or was she still merely seeking her own happiness and inner peace, knowing now that these could only be found in Jesus? Was it a mixture of both? These are very important questions for us all to ask ourselves. The more we understand the truth about our own heart and our relationship to Jesus, the more we can cooperate with his grace. If we have had a conversion in the past, we may well have first come back to Jesus simply seeking forgiveness, or perhaps healing, or help with our problems, or inner peace, or eternal life; but has this initial desire since become pure love for Christ and a desire to serve him simply because he deserves to be served? Do we love him sincerely for his own sake or are we still merely seeking something from him? This question no doubt would return to the heart of Magdalene in the years after the Ascension of Christ, as she would ponder her experience of the Saviour and ever discover new and deeper layers of meaning in the words he had once addressed to her. Holiness is to a large extent a matter of purifying the intention of our hearts. What do you seek from Jesus? This question is worthy of being pondered by us all. Magdalene's initial gratitude for the mercy of Christ no doubt matured into deep love for him, but has this also been our own experience?

"Mary"

The Good Shepherd knows his sheep by name and how sweet it was for Mary Magdalene to hear her name pronounced by Christ on Easter Sunday. "Mary!" In all human history was there ever as much joy transmitted by one single word? It was the full joy of the Resurrection in an instant. It was hope for a world that thought it was destined to hopelessness. It was indescribable supernatural peace and joy to the soul of Magdalene. Life was worth living again. This one word brought beauty back to the world. It was as though the birds had stopped singing and the sun had grown dimmer since the hour he closed his eyes on the Cross, but now the world was ablaze with glory once again. But above all, when her name was pronounced, it was the love in his voice that she could feel penetrating into the depths of her being. In that one word he said: "Mary I love you. I will never forget you and I personally wanted to come and bring you my peace. Everything is going to be all right. You can rejoice now and nothing will ever take that joy from you again. I have come to you that my own joy may be in you, and that your joy may be full (Jn 15:11). The evil of the world is conquered! Death is now nothing but transition! It has no real power over you anymore. Thank you for standing by me in all my trials. Your future is full of hope. I have prepared a happiness for you that you cannot even begin to imagine." What a heavenly joy it is to hear the Risen Lord Jesus call us by name! He knows each one of us personally. He knows every little detail of our lives. He knows our past, our fears, our wounds, our joys, our desires, our loves. He cares about us and wants only to heal us and make us happy. If we would only abandon ourselves to him like Magdalene, his joy would be in us and our joy would be complete.

Turning toward the Lord

In the empty tomb Mary had to turn twice in order to see the Risen Lord. She turned a first time but for some reason she did not recognise him. Was it that she was blinded by the rising sun at his back? Or was it that she was simply prevented from recognising him, as were the disciples of Emmaus? It is a mystery. We also have to make a double "interior turn" toward the Risen Lord in order to recognise him today, truly present in the Eucharist. We have already "turned" to the Lord Jesus once, so to speak; we go to Mass and come into his Real Presence in the Eucharist so often, but have we made that second interior turn which allows us to truly see him present behind the eucharistic veil? We have to turn toward him not with the senses, not just with our physical vision, but with the vision of the heart. We need to pray to the Holy Spirit to anoint the faculties of our souls, that our intellect may have the spiritual vision of a faith that pierces the eucharistic appearances and glimpses the Face of the Risen Lord. We all need to have this holy shock of the Real Presence, the moment in which we come to know truly that Christ is present in the Blessed Sacrament. This is a moment that changes our entire lives and opens our souls to a new outpouring of grace and of Easter joy. Saint John Paul II called it "Eucharistic amazement".[3] We should not just say: "Jesus rose from the dead two thousand years ago" as though it were an event confined to the past, but rather "Jesus is risen!"

The Risen Conqueror is alive and present in the Blessed Sacrament today and he waits for you! Thanks to the eucharistic mystery, the Resurrection is now! Every day upon our altars the sacramental species is raised up from being dead matter into becoming the living presence of him who sits at the right hand of the Father. Do you understand how good this news is? If you were to let this

---

[3] Pope John Paul II, *Ecclesia de Eucharistia*, no. 6.

truth take hold of your heart, I think you would drop this book right now and run like Mary Magdalene to your nearest adoration chapel! Then my mission would be truly accomplished and a new phase of your life would begin.

In my life there is a before and an after in relation to the moment in which I first had the astonishing experience of the truth of the Real Presence of Jesus in the Eucharist. It was a grace I received after a sincere prayer addressed to the Most Blessed Virgin Mary. She is the one through whom God grants this most beautiful of all graces. I think that when a soul is counted worthy of going straight to heaven at death, it will look back and realise that the life of heaven actually began in the moment that it truly discovered the Blessed Sacrament. The hope that this encounter with the eucharistic Lord brings is strong enough to heal us of all of our fears in this valley of sorrow. There have even been therapists who have prescribed a holy hour as therapy to anxious patients and witnessed astounding results. No matter how big our problems may seem, the One who has the power to solve them all is present right now in the Eucharist. All those who discover this "Hidden Manna" will never be conquered by the darkness of evil. They see the Light of the World! Here is how Pope Benedict, inspired by Saint Edith Stein, described the attitude one should have toward the presence of the Risen Lord in the Blessed Sacrament:

> The hidden treasure, the good greater than any other good, is the Kingdom of God—it is Jesus himself, the Kingdom in person. In the sacred Host, he is present, the true treasure, always waiting for us. Only by adoring this

presence do we learn how to receive him properly—we learn the reality of communion, we learn the Eucharistic celebration from the inside. Here I would like to quote some fine words of Saint Edith Stein, Co-Patroness of Europe, who wrote in one of her letters: "The Lord is present in the tabernacle in his divinity and his humanity. He is not there for himself, but for us: for it is his joy to be with us. He knows that we, being as we are, need to have him personally near. As a result, anyone with normal thoughts and feelings will naturally be drawn to spend time with him, whenever possible and as much as possible." Let us love being with the Lord! There we can speak with him about everything. We can offer him our petitions, our concerns, our troubles. Our joys. Our gratitude, our disappointments, our needs and our aspirations.[4]

What could be more normal for one who truly believes in the eucharistic Presence of Christ than to go and spend as much time with him as he possibly can? We should try to cling to his presence with love, in the same way that Magdalene did, as soon as she knew it was really him. In fact, the implication of what Saint Edith Stein and Pope Benedict are saying, is that it would be a little abnormal or unnatural to have no interest in going to behold Jesus, really present in the Blessed Sacrament. It would manifest a problem of faith or at least of understanding and feeling. If we do not get excited about the Real Presence of Christ in the Blessed Sacrament then perhaps the full significance of this truth has not yet fully sunk into our minds and hearts. Today people literally spend hours

---

[4] Pope Benedict XVI, Marian Vespers with the seminarians of Bavaria, Altötting, September 11, 2006.

every day wasting their time in front of a television or computer screen. How different the Church and the world would be, if we would only give that time to adoration of the living eucharistic King!

Go!

"Go to my brethren and say to them, I am ascending to my Father and your Father, to my God and your God" (Jn 20:17). In his most celebrated book entitled *Life of Christ*, the Venerable Archbishop Fulton Sheen adheres to the traditional portrait of Saint Mary Magdalene as the penitent sister of Martha. It is a marvel of divine election that this once sinful woman was nonetheless commissioned to be the first missionary of the Risen Lord. Sheen heralds her as the one chosen to break open for the world the sweet news of the Resurrection of Jesus Christ, just as she had broken open the alabaster jar which announced the arrival of his death. The great archbishop who was himself a true apostle of the Risen Lord speaks beautifully of the "Apostle to the Apostles" as she arrives at the empty tomb on Easter Sunday:

> The idea of the Resurrection did not seem to enter her mind either, though she herself had risen from a tomb sealed by the seven devils of sin. Finding the tomb empty, she broke again into a fountain of tears . . . Poor Magdalene! Worn from Good Friday, wearied by Holy Saturday, with life dwindled to a shadow and strength weakened to a thread, she would "take Him away." Three times did she speak of "Him" without defining His name. The force of love was such as to suppose no one else could

possibly be meant. Jesus said to her: Mary. That voice was more startling than a clap of thunder. She had once heard Jesus say that He called His sheep by name. And now to that One, Who individualized all the sin, sorrow, and tears in the world and marked each soul with a personal, particular, and discriminating love, she turned, seeing the red livid marks on His hands and feet, she uttered but one word: "Rabboni!" (which is the Hebrew for "Master"). Christ had uttered "Mary" and all heaven was in it. It was only one word she uttered, and all earth was in it. After the mental midnight, there was this dazzle; after hours of hopelessness, this hope; after the search, this discovery; after the loss, this find. Magdalene was prepared only to shed reverential tears over the grave; what she was not prepared for was to see Him walking on the wings of the morning. To the honor of womanhood it must forever be said: A woman was closest to the Cross on Good Friday, and first at the tomb on Easter Morn. Mary was always at His feet. She was there as she anointed Him for burial; she was there as she stood at the Cross; now in joy at seeing the Master, she threw herself at His feet to embrace them . . . She was to break the precious alabaster box of His Resurrection so that its perfume might fill the world.[5]

An angelic vocation

In commenting upon her life and upon this apostolic mission which the Risen Jesus bestows upon Mary Magdalene, Saint Thomas Aquinas concludes that in spite of her past, she has now been elevated to some kind of "angelic"

[5] Fulton J. Sheen, *Life of Christ* (New York: Doubleday, 1977), pp. 591–94.

dignity. Not only was her love and adoration angelic, but her mission is also of an angelic nature. In Greek the word "angel" signifies a messenger sent by God himself for some important mission. Magdalene's message is the most important one humanity has ever heard. Thanks to the Resurrection of the Lord, the world now has a hope that nothing can destroy. Now suffering has meaning and death has lost its frightening power. She is the first person in human history chosen to announce this sublime message of the Resurrection of Jesus Christ and she is also the prophetess of his Ascension (Jn 20:17). All along she has been prophesying by her gestures, now she is commanded to prophesy with words too.

John the Baptist was the prophet chosen to proclaim to the world the arrival of the Lamb of God who will take away its sin. Mary Magdalene was the one chosen to reveal the same Lamb of God through the prophetic gestures of her love. When, as a repentant sinner, she first threw herself at his feet and received the happy news of the divine mercy, she was showing to Israel the one who was taking her sins and the sins of the world upon himself. When again she threw herself at his feet during the banquet of Bethany, she was prophesying the arrival of the moment when those sins would be nailed to the Cross and buried in the tomb forever. During the public life of Christ she was a mysterious prophetess of mercy, chosen for the sweetest of all missions: to love Christ in a radical way and to be the instrument through which the merciful love in the heart of Christ was revealed to the world. But now as the sins of the world have at last been washed away and as the Victor emerges triumphant from his war on the powers of hell, her prophetic tidings must find a voice. She is the first true messenger of the gospel, for the Good News was not complete until the moment of the Resurrection. Just as the Baptist prepared Israel for the visitation of the Messiah, Magdalene is now chosen to prepare the hearts of the apostles themselves for the visitation of the Risen Lord.

Throughout the Gospel, in almost every text in which she appears, Magdalene has been criticised by others but defended and praised by Christ. Now as she announces the joy of the Resurrection to the apostles, many of them doubt the truth of her message and when Jesus finally appears he rebukes them for not trusting in the words of Magdalene (Mk 16:14). Even after the Resurrection Jesus is still defending this dearly beloved consoler of his heart. Christ is always on the side of those who know how to love him sincerely. It is love alone that merits the choicest blessings from the Lord. Adorers are often given the most sublime missions by Jesus but he only bestows this dignity because he knows that, like Magdalene, they would rather be clinging to his feet than doing any other thing. "Now is not the time to cling to me, but go" (Jn 20:17). When they go out into the world to evangelise, faithful adorers seek the glory of Christ and not their own. They want nothing but to gaze upon his eucharistic face and contemplate his life, but at times they know they are being sent by him to fulfil some apostolic task. As soon as it is done they will be back at his feet and under the light of the monstrance once again.

Here is how Saint Thomas describes the angelic dignity of the "Apostle to the Apostles":

Notice the three privileges given to Mary Magdalene. First, she had the privilege of being a prophet because she was worthy enough to see the angels, for a prophet is an intermediary between angels and the people. Secondly, she had the dignity or rank of an angel insofar as she looked upon Christ, on whom the angels desire to look. Thirdly, she had the office of an apostle; indeed, she was an apostle to the apostles insofar as it was her task to announce our Lord's resurrection to the disciples. Thus, just as it was a woman who was the first to announce the words of death, so it was a woman who would be the first to announce the words of life.[6]

~

[6] Thomas Aquinas, *Commentary on the Gospel of John*, 2519.

Conclusion

A study of the life of Saint Mary Magdalene is a source of profound encouragement. We can only marvel to see such a poor broken sinner rising from darkness in an explosion of love for Christ and then running with the greatest confidence along the way of perfection. She emerges from the desperate ruins of her life and becomes heaven's champion of love. So pleasing was she to the heart of Christ that she is chosen to announce his Resurrection to the apostles themselves. He would come to them in his risen glory in his own time but he wanted the way to be prepared first by an angel of love. If Jesus chose her for this singular privilege it was to give us all hope. The first apostle of the Resurrection is not a soul who had been pure and perfect from childhood but rather a poor broken sinner from whom were expelled seven demons. None of us can say that we are not potential candidates for canonisation, regardless of what we may have done in the past. She is hope for sinners and thanks to her we know that though our sins be as scarlet, in Christ we can become whiter than snow. If we follow the path of love traced out by the Apostle to the Apostles then at the moment of death we will be able to go in peace to the One who is the friend of sinners.

"Noli me tangere . . ."

When the remains of Saint Mary Magdalene were exhumed in Saint Maximin in the Middle Ages, a startling discovery awaited those commissioned for the task by King Charles of Anjou. As the precious treasures of her bones were unearthed, and the skull of one who had been present on Calvary and in the empty tomb was examined, the trembling witnesses observed something very mysterious. On the forehead of the saint there was a piece of her holy flesh that had not fully undergone corruption. It did not seem to be entirely incorrupt either, but in spite of the centuries that had passed, some trace of her flesh still remained there. Tradition has it that on the morning of the Resurrection, when the Risen Lord told Magdalene not to cling to him or *"Noli me tangere"* as it is translated in Latin, that he gently touched her forehead with his risen finger. The flesh that came into contact with the incorrupt hand of the Saviour could not undergo corruption in the same way as the rest of her mortal body. This mysterious relic of the saint's body is still preserved in the Basilica in Saint Maximin, in what is known as the *"Noli me tangere"* reliquary.

When the Roman persecutions finally came to an end, a church was constructed on the spot of her tomb and the fourth century alabaster sarcophagus, which remains to this day, was imported from Rome to house the precious relics. Eventually this church was completely destroyed by the Saracen invaders and the relics of the saint disappeared under the rubble. But in the thirteenth century, the king of the region demanded that excavations be carried out until this spiritual treasure was relocated. The upper part of her skull and some of her bones were eventually found, hidden in another sarcophagus along with the inscription: "here lies the body of Blessed Mary Magdalene" and an explanation of how the relics had been hidden so as to protect them from the invaders. The king brought the discovery to the Holy Father in Rome, knowing that since the early centuries the jawbone of the saint had been entrusted to the Pope and was jealously preserved in the Church of Saint John Lateran. The Holy Father, Pope Boniface VIII, put the jawbone and the skull together and found that there was a perfect match. There was no doubt in his mind that these were the bones of the Apostle to the Apostles and so in 1295 he published a papal bull announcing that the authentic relics of Saint Mary Magdalene had been rediscovered and granting indulgences to all who would make the pilgrimage to Saint Maximin.[1] So overjoyed was King Charles of Anjou by this rediscovery that he began the construction of a magnificent basilica, the grandeur of which could only be paralleled in Rome or Paris, there in the small town of Saint Maximin. Even today the enormous basilica still dominates the local landscape. The basilica became a place of extraordinary documented miracles and continues to be the most popular religious sanctuary of Provence. The Dominicans were entrusted by the Pope with the care of the basilica and they made of it their French noviciate for almost seven hundred years. Today it is in the custody of the Missionaries of the Most Holy Eucharist.

---

[1] Étienne-Michel Faillon, *Monuments inédits sur l'apostolat de Marie Madeleine* (Paris: Ateliers Catholiques du Petit-Montrouge, 1848), p. 819.

The nearby grotto where the saint spent her last years in contemplation is also an important place of pilgrimage and prayer. Saint John Cassian (A.D. 360–435), an Eastern Father of the Church and a founder of monastic communities, heard of the contemplative ending to the beautiful life of Mary Magdalene upon his arrival in Gaul. Even though Christianity had been illegal and persecuted for the first three centuries, the site of Magdalene's final abode had always been commemorated by a small oratory and visited often by the local Christians. Now that Christianity had emerged from the catacombs, Cassian made his pilgrimage to Provence and was led by the local Christians to the holy grotto. The saint was so stunned by the supernatural beauty of the place that he established a monastic community in the very grotto itself. This man of God, who would profoundly influence Saint Benedict himself, brought the best in Egyptian monasticism to the West and *la Sainte Baume* soon became one of the most important religious sites in France. The Cassianite monks remained present there until they were massacred by the Saracens in the eighth century. They were soon replaced by the Benedictines and eventually by the Dominicans who are still present at the site of the grotto of Saint Mary Magdalene to this day.

Eucharistic martyr of love

A beautiful story is told of how Saint Patrick, the Apostle to the Irish, once prepared two young noblewomen in the diocese of Elphin, Ireland, to receive their first Holy

Communion. He spoke to them with such fervour about the Real Presence of Christ in the Eucharist that when the solemn moment of their first Holy Communion arrived, these two young women were so enflamed with love that their souls departed from their bodies in an ecstasy and immediately entered the courts of heaven. These two eucharistic martyrs of love are known as Saints Eithne and Fidelma. Saint Mary Magdalene did not die in the moment of her first Holy Communion, but tradition tells us that Holy Communion was always a time of mystical ecstatic experiences for the saint. In her thanksgiving after Communion, the earthly angel of love would be elevated from this earth to taste the delights of the angelic hosts of heaven. It was fitting that her frail body should finally give up her fiery spirit during one such experience. In the two anointing scenes, when her attitude of love was praised as exemplary by Christ himself, it was on both occasions in the context of a banquet. Was she not perhaps always destined to teach us something about the attitude we should bring to the eucharistic banquet? The gratitude, contrition, adoration and love we see in those scenes were probably pale foretastes of the attitude she would have at the time of Holy Communion. It was only natural that for her the life of heaven should begin through the mystery of the Eucharist. There is a direct continuity between what happens in Holy Communion and what will be our joy for eternity. There could not possibly be a more beautiful way to die than in the moment when the King of Love is present within us in the flesh. We do not know the precise details of her passing from this life, but the memory of Provence has never forgotten the essential part of the story. It was the Bread of Angels that swept her soul away from the peace of Sainte Baume into the peace of the promised land.

Magdalene merited such a holy death because she had been a true martyr of love. The pain she knew because of contrition for her sins and the pain she experienced as she watched streams of blood flow from the brow of her beloved Lord, understanding that there was a mysterious connection between her sins and his blood, became for her soul a sword akin to the one that was already piercing the soul of the Mother whose hand she held on Calvary. When the outpouring of the Holy Spirit came upon her at Pentecost she received the grace to meditate even more deeply on the Passion of Christ and the role in it of the Blessed Virgin whom she had been privileged to accompany through it all. How her heart grew in love and admiration for the Woman clothed in the light of Christ. Now that she could no longer see the face of Jesus with her physical eyes, she could still see him reflected in the face of Mary and not only because of the likeness of features. Her appearance was always discreet, but since Pentecost, the soul of the Virgin seemed to be transfigured by an even more heavenly light. However, even during these joyful beginnings of the life of the Church, Magdalene would still notice that the mind of the Virgin often seemed to wander back to Calvary and abundant tears could still be seen streaming from her face.

Magdalene would do all she could to recall the joy of the Resurrection while in her presence, but the wound of the Cross ran deep in our Lady's heart and at times while she was in prayer she seemed to be reliving the experience of the Crucifixion. It was from her that Mary Magdalene learned that even though the Passion was over, it should still live on in contemplation, in the Mystical Body of Christ. Magdalene would also weep bitter tears as she went back in spirit with the Virgin Mary to the painful scenes of Good Friday. In the anguished haste of persecution and exile she would one day have to be separated from that maternal heart she loved so much, for Providence had chosen her to implant her love for Christ into the soil of the Church in Europe; but never would Mary Magdalene forget the indescribable pain she had seen on the faces of Jesus and Mary on Calvary.

Even joyful meditation upon the Resurrection and the moment in which the cold, lifeless body she had helped lay in the tomb came back to life in an earth-splitting surge of divine power, could never entirely erase the bitter memory of the price paid for her sins. Even on his risen glorious body she had noticed that there were still some trace of his wounds, as though to remind her not to forget them. Although she was profoundly happy and at peace in the depths of her heart, her life became a bittersweet contemplation of the Passion, Death and Resurrection of Jesus. She saw this as the natural extension of her vocation to love Christ in a radical way during his mortal life. She was powerless to repay the Lord for his goodness to her, all she could do was to continue to love him radically through prayer. For the remaining decades of her holy existence and amidst the activities and adventures life threw at her, she would try to spend as much time as possible contemplating the memory of Jesus with all of the fervent love of her undivided heart. This would permit her to bear the burden of earthly life, in anticipation of the life of heaven. Eventually this love for Christ led her away from the crowds and to the lonely grotto of Sainte Baume where she could peacefully end her days in a life of perpetual pondering of the Paschal Mystery. Alone in the silence of her newly discovered "Mount of Olives" she would weep rivers of tears for her own sins and those of the whole world; and for what these sins had done to the immaculate flesh of her beloved Jesus. As though to confirm that there was no more reparation left to be made and that the passionate love of her heart was a holocaust accepted by heaven, the eucharistic Lord came personally in the end to carry her soul directly into the presence of the Father. She passed from an earthly ecstasy to the heavenly ecstasy, scarcely noticing the purification of death *en route*. Such a soul needed no more purification, for she had been dead to the world for decades.

For Magdalene, life was Christ and death was gain (Phil 1:21).

> Whom have I in heaven but you?
>　And there is nothing upon earth that I
> 　　desire besides you.
> My flesh and my heart may fail,
> 　but God is the strength of my heart and
> 　　my portion forever . . .
> But for me it is good to be near God. (Ps 73:25–28)

The life of Saint Mary Magdalene, which once seemed to be the greatest of failures to all of Israel, was in the eyes of all of heaven a success of the highest order. In heaven her life is remembered and honoured as that of an earthly angel of love!

Bibliography

Aquinas, Thomas. *Catena Aurea*. Vol. 4, Part 1. Translated by John Henry Newman. Eugene, Ore.: Wipf and Stock, 2005.

———. *Commentary on the Gospel of John*. Translated by Fabian Larcher and James Weishepl. Edited by Daniel Keating. Washington, D.C.: Catholic University of America Press, 2010.

Bruckberger, Raymond, O.P. *Marie Madeleine*. Paris: La Jeune Parque, 1953.

De Bérulle, Pierre. *Élévation sur Sainte Madeleine*. Paris: Éditions du Cerf, 1987.

Emmerich, Anne Catherine. *Mary Magdalen in the Visions of Anne Catherine Emmerich*. North Carolina: TAN Books, 2005.

Faillon, Étienne-Michel. *Monuments inédits sur l'apostolat de Marie-Madeleine*. Paris: Ateliers Catholiques du Petit-Montrouge, 1848.

Fernandez, Andres. *The Life of Christ*. Westminster, Md.: Newman Press, 1958.

Feuillet, André. "Les Deux Onctions Faites sur Jésus, et Marie-Madeleine", *Revue Thomiste*, LXXV (1975).

Frossard, André. *Dieu existe, je l'ai rencontré*. Paris: Fayard, 1976.

Gobi, Jean. *Les Miracles de Sainte Marie-Madeleine*. Paris: CNRS Éditions, 2009.

Goodier, Alban. *The Public Life of Jesus Christ*. New York: P.J. Kenedy & Sons, 1931.

Hardon, John, S.J. *The Treasury of Catholic Wisdom*. San Francisco: Ignatius Press, 1995.

Kowalska, Faustina, *The Diary: Divine Mercy in My Soul*. Stockbridge, Mass.: Marian Press, 2003.

Lacordaire, Henri. *Sainte Marie-Madeleine*. Paris: Éditions du Cerf, 2009.

Lagrange, M.J. *L'Évangile selon saint Jean*. Paris: Victor Lecoffre, 1925.

Monti, James. *The King's Good Servant but God's First*. San Francisco: Ignatius Press, 1997.

Newman, John Henry. *Discourses Addressed to Mixed Congregations*. London: Longmans, Green, and Co., 1906.

Sanson, Pierre. *Marie-Madeleine, celle qui a beaucoup aimé*. Paris: Albin Michel, 1934.

Sheed, Frank. *To Know Christ Jesus*. San Francisco: Ignatius Press, 1992.

Sheen, Fulton. *Life of Christ*. New York: Doubleday, 1977.

Teresa of Avila. *The Way of Perfection*. Translated and edited by E. Allison Peers. New York: Image Books, 1964.